Beyond the
Dot.coms

Beyond the Dot.coms

The Economic Promise of the Internet

ROBERT E. LITAN

ALICE M. RIVLIN

INTERNET POLICY INSTITUTE

BROOKINGS INSTITUTION PRESS
Washington, D.C.

Copyright © 2001

THE BROOKINGS INSTITUTION

1775 Massachusetts Avenue, N.W., Washington, D.C. 20036

www.brookings.edu

Library of Congress Cataloging-in-Publication data

Litan, Robert E., 1950–
Beyond the dot.coms : the economic promise of the Internet / Robert E.
Litan, Alice M. Rivlin.
  p. cm.
Includes bibliographical references and index.
  ISBN 0-8157-0002-4 (cloth : alk. paper)
  1. Internet—Economic aspects—United States—Forecasting. 2.
Industrial productivity—United States. 3. Labor productivity—United
States. I. Rivlin, Alice M. II. Title.
  HE7583.U6 L58 2001
  338'.06'0973—dc21   2001005704

9 8 7 6 5 4 3 2 1

The paper used in this publication meets minimum requirements of the
American National Standard for Information Science—Permanence of Paper
for Printed Library Materials: ANSI Z39.48-1992.

Typeset in Adobe Garamond

Composition by Oakland Street Publishing
Arlington, Virginia

Printed by R. R. Donnelley and Sons
Harrisonburg, Virginia

Foreword

THE DOT.COM STOCK market bubble has burst, and hundreds of Internet companies have gone under. Nevertheless, the economic benefits of the Internet revolution are likely to be significant. That is the conclusion of this brief guide to the economic impact of the Internet.

This book draws on the work of the Brookings Task Force on the Internet, which pulled together eight teams of experts from leading business schools and universities to study the possible impact of the Internet on major sectors of the U.S. economy over the next five years. Their papers, published in *The Economic Payoff from the Internet Revolution* (2001), constitute the most comprehensive and detailed examination yet of this important issue.

In *Beyond the Dot.coms*, Robert Litan and Alice Rivlin bring the conclusions of the task force's work to a wider audience and set the findings in a broader context: explaining the importance of productivity growth and how the Internet is likely to enhance it, and discussing the factors that are likely to influence both the amount of the expected productivity benefits and the pace at which they are likely to be realized. They also discuss the likely nonquantifiable economic benefits of the Internet—such as the added convenience and choice it affords all users.

The key conclusion of this study is that it is a fundamental mistake to equate the benefits of the Internet with the economic health of the dot.coms, or even of the broader "New Economy" technology sector. Instead, the real gains from the "Net" are likely to arise from its use by increasing numbers of firms and consumers throughout the rest of the so-called Old Economy.

Robert Litan is vice president, director of economic studies, and the Cabot Family Chair in Economics at Brookings. Alice Rivlin is a senior fellow in economic studies at Brookings, as well as Henry Cohen Professor at the New School University.

The authors are deeply indebted to the members of the Brookings Task Force on the Internet, who provided much of the analytical basis for this book, as well as much helpful guidance to the authors. The authors are also grateful for the very useful comments and suggestions of Alan Blinder, Robert Crandall, Catherine Mann, David Post, and Hal Varian; to Samara Potter for her excellent research assistance; to Alicia Dorsey Jones for secretarial assistance; to Catherine Theohary for verification; and to Martha Gottron for editing.

Finally, the authors and Brookings gratefully acknowledge the financial and intellectual support of the Internet Policy Institute.

As with all Brookings publications, the views expressed in this book are those of the authors and should not be ascribed to the trustees, officers, or other staff members of the Institution.

MICHAEL H. ARMACOST
President

October 2001
Washington, D.C.

Contents

Beyond the
Dot.coms

1

Is the Internet a Big Deal?

IN THE FEW years since its public launching in the mid-1990s, the Internet has proved to be a cheap, convenient, quick, and flexible means of communication for millions of people engaged in all kinds of activities. E-mail has become the standard form of communication within and among companies. Distant relatives and groups of teenage pals keep in touch on the net. Law enforcement officers use it to catch criminals. People with esoteric hobbies find each other. Churches, clubs, and community groups keep in touch with their members on the Internet. The net can be used to do research, check the weather, send invitations, make payments, trade stocks, reserve theater tickets, express opinions, listen to music, and buy or sell just about anything.

Another fast, cheap means of communication is certainly a nice thing to have, but will it fundamentally alter the way the American economy functions? Will average people have a higher standard of living in a few years because the Internet has made the economy more productive? Or will the Internet prove to be just one more way of sending messages—an alternative to phone or fax or mail—that has little fundamental impact on our well-being?

There is no shortage of strong opinions on the significance of the Internet. In the late 1990s the media were full of rash hyperbole predicting that information technology (IT) in general and the Internet in particular were creating a new economy. In this new economy incomes would grow more rapidly, stock values would soar, and recessions would be mild and infrequent. Confidence in the future of electronic commerce produced an explosion of new companies—the dot.coms—that attracted optimistic investors and turned young entrepreneurs into instant millionaires, at least on paper. Skeptics urged caution, but confidence in the future of the Internet ran high, and the stocks of dot.com companies soared—for a time. Then the bubble burst. Investors lost confidence in dot.coms with vague prospects but no profits. Dot.com stocks plummeted, as did stocks of Internet technology suppliers, and many dot.coms went bankrupt. The skeptics crowed that they had been proved right, and some voices predicted an "Internet depression" with prolonged distress in the world economy caused by the bursting of the Internet bubble in the United States.[1]

In this book we try to steer clear of both the hype and the gloom. Our aim is to present as realistic a picture as possible of the potential impact of the Internet on the U.S. economy over the next few years. We focus primarily on the Internet's potential effect on productivity growth (increase in output per hour worked), because productivity growth is the principal determinant of the rate at which the nation's standard of living increases.

As we discuss in greater detail in chapter 2, productivity growth is both variable and hard to predict. Productivity grew rapidly (almost 3 percent a year) in the United States from the end of World War II until 1973 and then slowed down unexpectedly. For more than two decades productivity grew at a sluggish pace, at about half its previous rate. Wages and the average standard of living grew slowly as well. Then, just as unexpectedly, in 1995 productivity growth began to accelerate back to something short of its previous rate—and the nation's standard of living accelerated with it.

Beginning in late 2000 the booming economy of the 1990s slowed, and in late 2001 it fell into recession. The big question now is whether the high rate of productivity growth enjoyed during the last half of the 1990s will resume when economic growth picks up again. Was the acceleration in productivity growth a temporary phenomenon associated with the particularly favorable combination of circumstances that prevailed in the second half of the 1990s? Or is there a good chance that the United States has moved to a high trend rate of productivity growth that may be sustained for some years to come? Part of the answer to this question turns on the impact the Internet will have on productivity growth during the next several years.

Because the Internet is so new and its impact on business is just beginning to manifest itself, we decided the best approach to projecting its effect would be to look closely at the nature of Internet use by companies and organizations at the leading edge in various sectors of the economy. To that end, we brought together a group of experts on various sectors of the economy to form the Brookings Task Force on the Internet. We asked these experts to analyze the productivity gains of the companies and organizations in their sectors that were using the net most intensively and then to estimate the impact on the sectors' productivity growth over the next five years, as these practices spread to other companies and organizations. The results of these studies are summarized in chapter 3. The studies themselves are brought together in a separate volume.[2]

The assignment we gave the sector experts was a daunting one, and their results must be regarded as educated guesses. Nevertheless, the answers were encouraging. The analyses indicate that the impact of the Internet on productivity in most sectors is just beginning but that it is likely to be significant. We believe that the Internet is likely to add roughly 0.25–0.50 percent a year to U.S. productivity growth (above what it otherwise would be) over the next five years. Perhaps surprising to some, virtually all of the impact will be on old economy sectors, including manufacturing, financial services, transportation, and retailing. Some of the impact also will come from cost reductions in noncommercial sectors, including government, health services, and education.

Much of the contribution of the Internet to productivity growth will arise not from new activities, but simply from faster, cheaper handling of information needed in ordinary business transactions, such as ordering, billing, and getting information to employees, suppliers, and customers. Information-intensive sectors, such as financial services, health services, and government are likely to see their transactions costs cut substantially. Some of the productivity improvement will come from firms using the Internet to manage supply chains more efficiently, improve scheduling, reduce inventories, and bring about more effective collaboration among different business partners. Increasing use of the Internet in a rapidly globalizing economy is likely to increase competition by broadening the reach of the market for both buyers and sellers. Increased competition may enhance productivity and may also shave profit margins. Ironically, the bursting of the Internet stock market bubble in 2000–01 may enhance its productivity-enhancing effects in the old economy as many former dot.commers take their skills to more conventional firms.

Not all of the economic benefits of the Internet will show up in productivity statistics. Consumers will benefit from increased convenience, a wider range of choices, and the opportunity to acquire products customized to their specifications. They may also benefit from fewer mistakes in processing information, which, in the case of improved accuracy of medical records, for example, may even save lives. In chapter 4, we discuss some of these hard-to-quantify benefits and why they are important even if they never enter the measured output of the economy.

How rapidly the potential economic benefits of the Internet are realized depends on three factors: width, depth, and speed. Increasing the width of the market of Internet users requires bridging the "digital divide," the invisible barrier that divides those who are comfortable with using computers and navigating the net from those who are not. Since the nonusers tend to be older, less educated, poorer, and minorities, bringing them into the Internet marketplace will take sustained and imaginative effort—one that may not fully play out for a generation.

Just because a company is using the net does not mean it has reorganized its operations at a depth necessary to take maximum advantage of the productivity-enhancing potential of the technology. Training employees to think differently and adapting business culture to take advantage of the Internet may well be more challenging than increasing the width of the Internet marketplace. Increasing the speed of the Internet, primarily by accelerating access to broadband connections, will also influence the realization of potential Internet benefits. So will resolution of policy issues involving security, privacy, intellectual property, and antitrust law. These issues are discussed in chapter 5.

In sum, we are optimistic about the future of the net and its effect on individual well-being. We believe that the impact of the Internet on the economy, while not as overwhelming as extreme cyber-enthusiasts claim, is likely to be positive, significant, and sustained. As we discuss in chapter 6, the impact of the Internet reaches well beyond the dot.coms. Indeed, the bursting of the dot.com bubble represents in part the failure of investors to realize that the importance of Internet technology lies primarily in its potential to improve the efficiency of the whole economy, not in new adventures in retail e-commerce. Similarly, while the Internet has certainly not abolished the business cycle or management miscalculation, it may help reduce inventory fluctuations. We see no evidence that the world is doomed to an Internet depression, but rather see far more light than darkness in the years ahead as the Internet revolution proceeds.

2 *Why Productivity Is So Important*

HOW MUCH IS the Internet likely to increase the standard of living of average Americans? That is the fundamental question this book addresses. To answer that question, we focus on the potential impact of the Internet on productivity growth, for the simple reason that productivity growth ultimately determines how fast the standard of living rises.

How much the whole economy can produce depends on how many hours the labor force is working and how productive those hours are. If there is full employment—that is, if almost everyone who wants to work has a job most of the time—then the total number of hours worked cannot change very much. Some people may change their minds about whether they want to work or not, and the amount of overtime or part-time work may vary some, but basically the total amount of time devoted to producing goods and services will change slowly because the size of the labor force changes slowly. In the United States the size of the labor force is currently growing about 1 percent a year. For the total output of the U.S. economy to grow faster than 1 percent a year, workers have to be producing more per hour worked; in other words, productivity has to be growing.

If productivity is growing, businesses will be making higher profits and can afford to pay higher wages, and, if unemployment is low, workers probably will be successful in obtaining those higher wages. Alternatively, wages may stay the same while increasingly productive companies compete with each other to sell more products by lowering their prices. If this happens, workers' real wages go up, because they can buy more. Either way, the productivity increase tends to be reflected in real wages, and hence in the standard of living.

Small changes in productivity growth make a huge difference if they are sustained for several years. If productivity grows at 3 percent a year, real per capita incomes will tend to double every twenty-four years; if productivity grows at half that rate, the standard of living will take twice as long to double.

Ways of Increasing Productivity

There are several ways to increase labor productivity. Perhaps the most obvious is giving workers more and better tools to work with—what economists call "capital deepening." Computers and Internet connections are just another set of sophisticated tools with the potential to increase the productive capacity of workers.

A second way to increase labor productivity is to improve workers' skills through education and training—what economists call "human investment." Capital deepening and human investment often go together because workers need new skills to handle more sophisticated equipment and perform more elaborate operations. Sometimes, however, machines make it possible for less-skilled people to do a job because the machine is doing the most demanding part of the work.

Sometimes an innovation—often an organizational or management breakthrough—increases the productivity of *both* labor and capital and produces an increase in what economists call "total factor productivity" because it cannot be identified with investments in either capital or labor. Such innovations are hard to pin down precisely because they are not associated with identifiable costs. Indeed, total factor productivity is sometimes just a fancy term for "we don't have a clue why this happened." The Internet, because its essential characteristic is linking different parts of the productive process, might be expected to increase total factor productivity.

Predicting Changes in Productivity Growth

Two dramatic changes, both unexpected, occurred in labor productivity growth in the United States during the last fifty years. As figure 2-1 shows, productivity grew rapidly from 1950 to 1973, averaging close to 3 percent a year. Explanations for this positive performance were not hard to find. World War II had left

Figure 2-1. *Average Annual Productivity Growth*

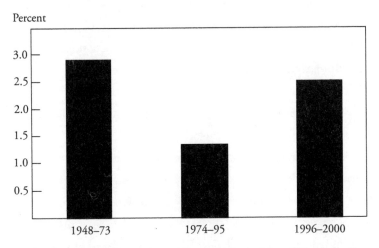

Percent

Source: Bureau of Labor Statistics, *Major Sector Productivity and Costs Index.* Data extracted on July 6, 2001, from http://stats.bls.gov/mlprhome.htm (public data query).

a legacy of rapid technological advances ready to be exploited for commercial purposes, as well as a large cohort of scientists and engineers able to turn their talents to civilian uses. The skills and education of the labor force increased significantly as returning soldiers took advantage of education and training benefits and as rising prosperity enabled young people to stay in school longer.

Whatever the reasons, the high rate of productivity growth and the increase in the standard of living that it made possible came to be widely regarded as normal. Then, after 1973, the rate of productivity growth plummeted unexpectedly and did not recover for more than twenty years (also shown in figure 2-1). The drop was first attributed to the rapid increase in oil prices and subsequent stagflation of the 1970s, but lower productivity growth persisted even after energy prices came down and macro-economic conditions improved. Other explanations, such as the inexperience of the large baby-boom generation that flooded into the labor force, the growth of environmental regulation, and the dearth of innovations in some industries, never convincingly explained the slowdown in productivity growth.

Again, whatever the reasons, the lower rate of productivity growth and the slower increase in real wages that went with it came to be regarded as "normal." Distinguished economists wrote books with titles like *The Zero Sum Society* (Lester Thurow) and *The Age of Diminished Expectations* (Paul Krugman) explaining the necessity of adjusting to slower growth. Then, again unexpectedly, beginning in 1996, productivity growth accelerated, increasing at 2.5 percent a year (see figure 2-1).[1] The more rapid growth persisted until the economy slowed abruptly in late 2000. As of this writing, it is not clear whether U.S. productivity growth has shifted to a higher trend—a new "normal" that will reassert itself when the economy speeds up again—or whether the high productivity growth will prove itself a short-lived phenomenon associated with conditions peculiar to 1996–2000.

Why Did Productivity Growth Accelerate?

Reasons for rapid acceleration of productivity growth in the mid-to-late 1990s remain mysterious, but the most likely explanation is that a lot of favorable factors came together at the same time. The economic stars were realigned.

The explosion of investment in computers and telecommunications technology was clearly a big part of the story, but the timing is mystifying. The computer and telecommunications revolution started much earlier and appeared, surprisingly, to have little impact on measured productivity for a long time. Indeed, the failure of widespread computer use to generate measurable productivity growth was puzzling to economists. As Robert Solow famously noted in 1987: "We see computers everywhere except in the productivity statistics."[2]

Dan Sichel, formerly of Brookings and now at the Federal Reserve Board, analyzed this problem in the mid-1990s and concluded that investment in computer equipment and software was simply not big enough in the period for which data were available, compared with the total capital stock, to have caused much of a visible increase in productivity growth.[3] By 2000, however, Sichel and his Fed colleague Stephen Oliner found that the rapid acceleration in productivity growth in the late 1990s was largely attributable to investment in communications as well as computer hardware and software (information technology, or IT): both the rapid increase in productivity in the manufacture of computers themselves, manifested in the rapidly rising power and falling prices of all kinds of information technology equipment, and the use of IT throughout the rest of the economy.[4] The same period also saw a rapid increase in the growth of total factor productivity, suggesting that the computer and telecommunications revolution (but not necessarily the Internet, or least not yet) was leading companies to reorganize their operations in ways that increased productivity by more than could be attributed to the investment in information technology itself.

Other analysts have used somewhat different methods and gotten somewhat different estimates, but there is a strong consensus that information technology was an important factor in the productivity surge of the late 1990s. Robert Gordon of Northwestern University has been the most outspoken skeptic, attributing most of the apparent productivity surge to cyclical factors, measurement changes, and the rapid increases in the efficiency within the technology sector itself, rather than to productivity gains stemming from the use of information technology in the rest of the economy. Even Gordon, however, in a more recent paper finds evidence that information technology use was contributing to an acceleration of productivity growth in the late 1990s.[5]

The President's Council of Economic Advisers in its annual report of 2001 marshaled additional evidence that information technology has propelled the productivity surge.[6] The council found that the labor productivity increase in 1995–99 was faster in sectors that were heavy IT users than in those that were not. The council also pointed out that most of the productivity growth in the second half of the 1990s was probably structural or long-run in nature, rather than cyclical. One recent analysis has essentially confirmed the council's analysis.[7]

Meanwhile, Paul David and other authors have counseled patience when assessing the impact of IT on productivity, based on experience with other major innovations in the past. David, in particular, notes that technological breakthroughs such as the electric motor typically do not significantly enhance productivity for many years after their invention, because it takes a long time for producers to change their operations and organization sufficiently to take advantage of the innovation.[8] Hence, it may have taken until the mid-1990s for IT to mature sufficiently to be really useful in production and for firms to become sophisticated enough to employ it effectively, and for competitive pressures to ensure that they did.

In any case, other factors also contributed to making the second half of the 1990s an unusually favorable time for the implementation of available technological innovation. Inflation was subdued and seemed likely to remain so, a circumstance that tends to lower long-term interest rates and make potential investors feel more comfortable about risking resources in major undertakings. At the same time, remarkably, unemployment rates had fallen to historically low levels, and employers were finding workers, especially skilled workers, increasingly hard to attract. Tight labor markets provided incentives for firms to substitute technology for workers, reorganize their operations to use employees more effectively, and help workers to increase their skills—all activities likely to raise productivity.

The favorable macroeconomic conditions of this period were partly a result of good luck and partly attributable to effective economic policy. The good luck on inflation included the rising value of the dollar, which sent import prices down; favorable commodity prices, especially energy prices, until the very end of the 1990s; and slow growth in medical care costs, as the nation shifted to a health care delivery system dominated by managed care. The Federal Reserve gets some of the credit for keeping inflation low, especially for raising short-term interest rates in 1994 when the economy appeared on the verge of overheating and for lowering them again in 1995 when the risk abated. Aggressive efforts on the part of both the executive branch and Congress to reduce the federal budget deficit, which ultimately succeeded in turning the deficit into a surplus, made the Federal Reserve's inflation fighting easier, put downward pressure on long-term interest rates, and improved the investment climate by demonstrating discipline in government.

The United States economy proved itself unusually flexible and competitive in the mid-1990s and hence well positioned to take advantage of the explosion of innovations occurring in computers and telecommunications. The highly competitive environment, in turn, reflected the cumulative effect of a long series of policies aimed at reducing regulation and moving toward freer trade. The aggressive restructuring of American industry in the face of global competition, beginning in the Rust Belt in the 1980s, also left a legacy of more nimble and competitive American companies. Business strategies aimed at fostering innovation, adaptability, and continuous productivity improvement became standard operating procedures. The explosive rise of the venture capital industry also fueled the creation of new companies that helped lead the IT revolution. All of these favorable factors in combination enabled the U.S. economy to respond in a way that turned innovation, especially in information technology, into a high rate of productivity growth sustained for more than five years.

Then, around the middle of 2000, the economy began to slow—precipitously, by the end of that year—while productivity growth dropped, as it always does when the economy slows. The slowing of the economy was partly a delayed result of interest-rate increases engineered by the Federal Reserve in an effort to slow the economy's growth. The Fed, worried that the economy was overheating and in danger of running out of workers and, consequently, that inflation was beginning to creep up and might accelerate, raised interest rates several times over nearly a year beginning in June 1999. At the time of the last increase in May 2000, the economy was still growing strongly, and the tighter monetary policy appeared not to be working. But when the slowdown came in the last quarter of 2000, it was sharper than the Federal Reserve had expected or intended, and its abrupt arrival took economists by surprise.

Delayed reaction to the Federal Reserve's restrictive monetary policy was only one of the explanations for the economy's rapid deceleration. Higher energy prices acted like a tax, requiring consumers and businesses to spend more for energy, leaving less to spend on other goods and services. The stock market dropped as investors became more realistic about future earnings, especially in technology companies. Consumption, which had been partly sustained by spending out of increased stock market wealth, slowed. Investment, especially in IT, took a dive. Overcapacity developed quickly, especially in technology-producing industries, and inventories of unsold merchandise rose. To no one's surprise, productivity growth slowed with the economy. Companies initially are reluctant to lay off workers when demand slackens, and excess workers mean measured productivity drops.

The catastrophic terrorist attack on the United States on September 11, 2001, compounded the negative factors already dragging on economic growth and threw the economy into recession. In the face of fear and uncertainty both consumers and investors reined in spending, and demand for all sorts of goods and services plummeted.

The big questions as we write this are how long the slowdown in the economy will last and what will happen to productivity growth when demand picks up again? Will productivity move back up to the growth path of the last half of the 1990s, or will it fall back to the lower rates of the previous twenty years? The answers to those questions will depend, in part, on the long-run productivity impact of the Internet, a subject dealt with in the next chapter.

3 Productivity and the Internet: What Lies Ahead?

ECONOMISTS HAVE A poor track record in forecasting changes in the rate of productivity growth. The problem of predicting the Internet's impact is especially difficult, because the Internet is such a new tool and its use in commercial transactions, while growing fast, is still tiny in relation to the whole economy. The volume of e-commerce is currently probably less than $200 billion in a $10 trillion economy. Not enough historical data have been accumulated yet to allow economists to use conventional statistical techniques to explain how the Internet has affected the economy in the past—let alone to serve as a basis for making projections into the future. Moreover, even if part of the surge in productivity growth in the late 1990s is attributable to the use of the Internet—an effect likely to be small given the recency of the net revolution—there is no way yet to disentangle the effect of the Internet from the effects of other aspects of information technology.

Hence, we decided that the best way to gather clues about the future impact of the Internet was quite straightforward—to look at what was going on and then try to project what would happen if the newest and most effective uses of the Internet were more widely adopted. Accordingly, we assembled a team of experts on particular sectors of the economy and asked them to examine how leading-edge firms or institutions in these sectors were using the Internet; what its impact on cost, prices, and productivity appeared to be; and how rapidly Internet usage might spread to other parts of the sector. The experts produced papers on their sectors and presented them in the fall of 2000 at a conference in Washington, where they had an opportunity to interact with each other and with critics of their methodology and estimates. The revised papers were collected in a volume, for which we wrote a summary.[1] That summary is the basis for this chapter.

The authors of the sector papers were asked to present enough background on the recent history and structure of the sector to give the reader a context for understanding their projections. In the most daunting part of the assignment, the authors were asked to provide their best estimates as to how the Internet might alter productivity in the sector over the next five years or so. These tasks were extremely challenging, and all of the authors protested that the Internet was such a new tool and its use evolving so rapidly that their estimates should not be construed as more than tentative guesses. Nevertheless, taken together, their work clearly indicates that the Internet has the *potential* to increase productivity growth in a variety of distinct, but mutually reinforcing, ways:

—by significantly reducing the cost of many transactions necessary to the production and distribution of goods and services;

—by increasing the efficiency of management, especially by enabling firms to manage their supply chains more effectively and to communicate more easily both within the firm and with customers and partners; and

—by increasing competition, making prices more transparent, and broadening markets for both buyers and sellers.

The authors reached these conclusions by surveying the available literature, conducting interviews with knowledgeable individuals in their respective sectors, and applying their own judgment in arriving at the quantitative estimates they were able to report (or more accurately, *ranges* of estimates). We did not have the resources to enable the authors to conduct in-depth surveys of their own or to collect new data from the firms or organizations in their sectors, although we wish we did. We are hopeful that researchers in the future will be able to do this. In the meantime, we believe these estimates provide a plausible set of "guestimates", informed by the judgment and experience of some of the most experienced researchers around, of the potential economic benefits of the Internet revolution.

In the balance of this chapter, we summarize some of the examples, drawn from the sector papers, of how these claims might prove true. We then do our best to add up the potential impacts suggested by the authors.

Reducing the Cost of Transactions

The most important attribute of the Internet also may be the most obvious: it provides a cheap way of transmitting a lot of information quickly and conveniently. Many routine transactions—making payments; processing and transmitting financial information; record keeping; search and analysis; ordering, invoicing, and recruiting; getting information to suppliers, employees, and customers—can simply be handled less expensively with web-based technology than on paper or in other electronic ways. Many firms, especially those in data-intensive industries such as financial services and medical care, can reduce their cost of production not by doing anything new or different—but just by doing the same things cheaper using Internet technology.

Within manufacturing firms, intranets (closed communications systems within organizations) and other web-based technology allow management to share information easily and cheaply across the organization and to cut the cost and improve the accuracy of accounting, ordering, tracking, invoicing, recruiting, and other routine functions. Net-based communications also enable employees in different parts of the firm to work together on product development, marketing, and other projects. Firms such as Cisco Systems and Oracle, which rely heavily on web-based technology for their internal communications and management, claim significant savings from this source.

Andrew McAfee of the Harvard Business School, who examined the manufacturing sector, projects that additional reductions in cost should materialize as more and more firms shift to web-based technologies for information flow and back-office functions, such as purchasing, invoicing, and payments. "While these activities are mundane and only rarely considered possible sources of competitive advantage, they still are time consuming and expensive to carry out in the absence of automation. In the Internet era, this automation is becoming readily available," McAfee writes.

Patricia Danzon and Michael Furukawa from the Wharton School at the University of Pennsylvania note that the potential for transactions cost savings from transition to the Internet is especially high in the health care sector, because it is so large (14 percent of gross domestic product, or GDP), so information-intensive, still so dependent on paper-based records, and so inefficient. Moving processing of health insurance claims from the current mix of paper and electronic data interchange (EDI) onto the Internet would require aggressive efforts to standardize claims formats, but savings could be large. EDI providers assert that they can reduce processing costs from $10–$15 for a paper claim to $2–$4 for an EDI claim. Web-based processors may be able to deliver the same service for less than $1 a claim. Perhaps as much as $27 billion a year could be saved if health insurance claims processing were shifted to the web, with improved speed and convenience thrown into the bargain.

Medical record management is another area in which the Internet offers great potential not only for cutting costs, but for improving the quality and effectiveness of care. In January 2001 the Department of Health and Human Services issued comprehensive rules protecting the privacy of individuals' medical records. It is still early to know if these regulations will constitute a significant barrier to the development of databases that can be accessed by a wide range of providers with appropriate authorization. But if such databases can be built and maintained, patients and providers would benefit enormously from conversion of current, mostly paper, medical records into an electronic medical record (EMR) in standard format. Health care providers would then be able to access a patient's full medical history quickly and enter their own observations and treatments. The instant availability of the EMR would save time for the patient as well as for the various providers, reduce the costs of sending records, and avoid duplicative or medically inconsistent treatment. The EMR would also be enormously valuable to individuals who require medical attention when they are away from home. Prescriptions also could be entered on the EMR and simultaneously sent directly to the pharmacy, reducing both cost and error rates in filling prescriptions. Of course, full utilization of the EMR by physicians requires standardization of formats and development of convenient handheld devices for entering treatment information and prescriptions easily as doctors walk around the hospital or office. These standards are now being developed, and investments in computerized personal assistants continue to grow.[2]

In the financial services arena, Eric Clemons and Loren Hitt, also from the Wharton School, argue that most of the savings from automating internal or back-office transactions already may have been realized in the pre-Internet era. Nonetheless, the net should enable financial institutions to lower their processing costs further, allowing customers to enjoy reduced waiting and travel time as well as mailing costs.

The economy as a whole could also realize substantial savings if online banking were to replace face-to-face transactions with bank tellers as well as the whole system of payment by check. Checks have to be sorted and transported back to their original writers—an archaic and expensive process compared with sending payments over the Internet (some estimates put the difference in cost at 10 to 1 or even higher). The transition to online small-value payments, however, may be slow. Many customers like interacting with a real person and continue writing checks not only out of habit, but also because the true costs of check use are not visible to them or because they regard a cancelled check as a tangible proof of payment not reliably replaceable by anything electronic. Hence, the need to maintain dual technologies for retail banking may limit the realization of the potential savings from online banking for some time.

Retail banking is an example of a major tension exhibited across the financial services industry. This tension is between financial services based on customer-provider relationships tied to geography and the provider's knowledge of the customer, on the one hand, and the savings offered by online markets for standard financial products that bypass traditional intermediaries, on the other. The tension is perhaps most evident in brokerage services, where the advent of the Internet has precipitated a split between the relationship-dependent services of investment advising and portfolio management and the standardized service of stock trading. Customers benefit from the lower transactions cost of online trading, if they are willing to do their own research and forgo advice, as well as from their ability to shop for lower commissions by searching the web. Some of the cost reduction is, however, offset by increased advertising and marketing costs as online brokers compete with other brokers. In any event, the market solution increasingly appears to be that firms will sell their brokerage and advice services separately (or the services will be supplied from separate firms).

In the mortgage lending industry customers are using the Internet to shop for information and compare rates, although only a tiny fraction of mortgages now originate online. This may change over the next few years, however, as consumers grow more comfortable using the newly authorized "digital signatures." As more mortgages are completed online, consumers will benefit from lower margins in this part of the business, plus lower costs in processing mortgage applications.

Another source of potentially significant savings in transaction costs, perhaps surprising to some, is found in the government sector. As Jane Fountain, of Harvard's Kennedy School of Government, notes in her study, governments at all levels spend substantial resources answering questions—where services can be obtained, who is eligible for benefits, what laws and regulations apply—or gathering information from citizens who want to report a pothole, apply for a permit, renew a license, or give their views on a public issue. The Internet has enormous potential, only beginning to be realized, for dispensing information to citizens less expensively and more accurately than telephone inquiries. A website can be updated more easily and cheaply than a paper publication and can be designed for quick, user-friendly retrieval of the information needed for a wide variety of purposes. In particular, filing tax returns online cuts costs both to the government and to the taxpayer, and the same can be said for filing many kinds of applications for benefits, permits, licenses, and the like. Building contractors can file architectural drawings online in many jurisdictions and avoid walking around from one government office to another with huge rolls of blueprints. Students can apply for scholarships and loans online; workers who lose jobs, for unemployment benefits; seniors, for retirement benefits and other services.

Fountain stresses that the e-government revolution nonetheless has a long way to go. Some state governments, such as Washington and Georgia, offer significant services on the Internet; others are only beginning to move into the digital age. Most federal agencies and local governments have just started to explore the Internet's potential usefulness to them. Realization of savings will be hampered—as it will in financial services—by the need to maintain alternative systems for those unable or unwilling to use the Internet. Moreover, ease of access to government information and services may generate more inquiries and more demands for service. To the extent that the Internet reduces the cost of interaction between government and the private sector, part of the benefit will show up in private sector productivity. Part will also be reflected in lower government expenditures and greater citizen satisfaction, neither of which enters explicitly into productivity statistics.

Education is also a large, information-intensive sector of the economy, where the long-run impact of information technology and the Internet may turn out to be considerable. Austin Goolsbee of the University of Chicago, however, expects that the impact of the Internet on education productivity in the next few years is likely to be slight. Distance-learning opportunities are growing at the postsecondary level and have the potential for saving students travel time and giving them a chance to learn at their convenience and at their own pace. But the Internet is only one tool of distance learning and so far has not been used very effectively. The greatest potential appears to be in developing interactive course material in subjects where drill and individual pacing pay off. These learning tools are expensive to develop, but once they are, they can be replicated and distributed on the net at close to zero marginal cost. Integration of such opportunities with other teaching methods could increase the productivity of education at several levels—notably in business schools and in executive education programs, where numerous e-education experiments are under way—but this process is likely to play out gradually.

The Internet and Efficient Management

So far these examples have focused on the Internet's potential for cutting the cost of information-intensive activities without necessarily reorganizing those activities to make them work better as well as cost less. The Internet may have even greater potential as a management tool, however. It may make possible changes in operations that enhance efficiency within firms and across partnerships and alliances in many sectors of the economy and may cause significant restructuring of those sectors in the process.

Many of the potential efficiency gains come from use of web-based technology to manage supply chains more effectively and reduce inventory. These savings may show up within the firm, from better scheduling or information-sharing across the company, or in more efficient interaction with other firms in the supply chain. As McAfee documents, Cisco Systems has been a leader in dealing with suppliers on the web to enhance the efficiency of its procurement. Indeed, Cisco has changed the definition of what it means to be a "manufacturer," since it outsources most of its manufacturing operations to other companies in its net-based supplier community. Some of the savings to Cisco come from competitive bidding by suppliers, which reduces the price to the buyer (but whose ultimate effects we view cautiously, as discussed later). The company also realizes savings from improved information flow and the ability to coordinate schedules to eliminate waiting and inventory accumulation at every stage. Cisco attempted to quantify the savings it derived from intensive use of the Internet as a management tool in the period 1995–99 and concluded that the cumulative savings amounted to more than 5 percent of its revenue in 1999—perhaps an upper-bound for such savings, which will not be attainable by many companies, but impressive nevertheless. As discussed later, McAfee uses this cost savings estimate to develop a range of projections for how effective the Internet will be more generally in reducing costs throughout the entire manufacturing sector.[3]

Other industries are also using the Internet effectively to link partners in joint enterprises across large distances, enabling partners to share production schedules and integrate their operations. One of the benefits of the closer linkage is speeding up decision-making when problems arise. The net-based information flow can reduce the phenomenon known as the "bullwhip effect," which arises when small changes in consumer demand are magnified by poor information flow and cause delays and inventory accumulation up the supply chain.

Charles Fine of MIT and Daniel Raff of the University of Pennsylvania examine the automobile industry—an important segment of manufacturing—and find multiple potential opportunities for Internet-aided increases in efficiency in this highly visible industry. They project productivity improvements in product development, procurement, and supply and in various aspects of the manufacturing process itself. They also explore the applicability to automobiles of the Dell model, under which customers specify exactly what features they want and the product is then built to their order and shipped directly from the factory. Fine and Raff also suggest that the automobile sector of the future will involve far fewer dealers and sales personnel than it does now.

Internet retailing has attracted a great deal of attention in the last few years. Much of the attention has focused on a few "pure play" retailers, such as Amazon.com and eBay, which sell only on the net. Joseph Bailey, of the University of Maryland, examined the retail sector, which constitutes about 9 percent of the economy. He concluded that although Internet sales are now only about 1 percent of total retail sales and are unlikely to account for more that 10 percent of retail revenues in five years, there is considerable potential for retailers using the Internet to increase efficiency. He does not expect much of the Internet's impact on retail efficiency to come from the pure play retailers, however. Rather, he anticipates that conventional retailers will increasingly use the net to manage their supply operations more effectively, bypass intermediaries, and reduce inventories. Conventional retailers, such as department stores, will also grow their Internet sales, using the Internet as an alternative way of reaching customers, along with catalogues and in-store sales. At the same time, the pure net retailers will add brick-and-mortar warehouses (Amazon.com has already taken this step) and become more like conventional retailers. A hybrid model will come to dominate retailing, in which almost all retail establishments use the net to communicate with and sell to customers, but few depend solely on Internet sales. And while all this is occurring, the retailing model pioneered by eBay—consumer-to-consumer commerce (C2C) via auctions on the net—is likely to continue to thrive.

Addressing a less visible sector of the economy, Anuradha Nagarajan and a team of researchers at the University of Michigan point out that the Internet is also in the process of radically transforming the trucking industry—or as it more accurately should be called, the logistics industry—which depends heavily on timely information for efficient operation. Customers need a low-cost way of finding the truck capacity they need when they need it and of comparing rates to get the best deal. Truckers need to find customers that will use their capacity fully so that they can avoid costly downtime and empty backhauls. The Internet is proving to be an inexpensive tool for matching these needs, and use of the Internet by both large and small trucking companies has risen rapidly since the mid-1990s. Traditional freight brokers are rapidly being replaced by electronic brokers, some set up by groups of carriers in search of the greater efficiencies made possible by integrating their fleets and schedules on the net.

Moreover, the Internet has made it possible for truckers to offer additional services to their customers, such as tracking shipments, rerouting them if necessary, and providing quick access to all relevant documentation. As a result, some trucking companies have been evolving into logistics managers offering a wide range of services customized to their users' particular needs. This transformation of traditional truckers into firms offering more comprehensive services makes it hard to identify the potential contributions of the Internet to productivity growth in the trucking sector narrowly defined. Greater efficiencies in transportation management ultimately will enhance the productivity of the many industries that use trucking services, and that is where the Michigan research team sees the greatest potential for Internet-related transportation savings.

Making Markets More Competitive

One of the major features of the Internet revolution is its potential to broaden the reach of markets and make at least part of the economy more competitive nationally and internationally. If prices of well-specified goods and services are posted on the net, buyers can shop for the best deal over a wide geographic area, even across international borders, and sellers can reach a larger group of potential buyers. The Internet has the potential to bring many markets—those in which products and services are "plain vanilla" and differ largely on the basis of price rather than quality—closer to the economists' textbook model of perfect competition, characterized by large numbers of buyers and sellers bidding in a frictionless market with perfect information. Moving markets in this direction should mean more efficient production, lower profit margins, and lower prices for consumers.

Another competitive benefit is likely to show up in online procurement. For a firm or hospital or government agency seeking to buy supplies, the Internet helps expand the range of bidders. Indeed, some firms and groups of firms have banded together to organize e-markets in hopes of lowering their costs, although, as McAfee points out, many of these markets are still not very sophisticated. Some e-markets are organized to encourage firms to pool their purchasing power to get the best deal from suppliers. The major automobile companies, as Raff and Fine note, are among the highest-profile examples of such joint efforts. Governments, as Fountain observes, are also beginning to use the Internet to pool their purchasing power.

The Internet will not always enhance competition, however. Given the importance of brand names—both off and on the net—it is quite likely that in some markets the net facilitates the rise of what economists call "monopolistic competition"—or competition between firms offering differentiated products and services. The net may make it easier for these firms to make their presence known and to distribute their wares or services. But it may not lead to textbook competition. In fact, some firms on the net will take advantage of the network externalities that are the central feature of the net to carve out substantial market shares that may be impervious, at least for a time, to effective erosion. The dominance of AOL in Internet access is one example.

Microsoft is endeavoring to carve out a similar dominant presence in Internet-delivered software and media services (and is taking on AOL at the same time).

In any event, to the extent the net broadens markets and makes them more transparent and competitive, consumers clearly benefit—but not all of the benefits flow from greater efficiency. Efficiency benefits occur when the Internet lowers barriers to competition by increasing the chances that a firm that develops a better product or a more efficient process or organizational structure can find its way into broader markets, win bids, sell its product, and exert pressure on its competitors to improve their efficiency. If, however, greater competition in a wider online marketplace simply cuts profit margins, consumers will benefit, but no productivity increase will have occurred.

Some of the high claims for productivity increase attributable to the Internet are suspect because they fail to distinguish between these two effects. A well-known study by two Goldman Sachs analysts projects large Internet-induced productivity gains in the manufacturing sector.[4] The two analysts believe that Internet markets will lower costs by eliminating various intermediaries. They also suggest that the profit squeeze among suppliers, induced by more intense competition in business-to-business, or B2B, Internet commerce, will lower procurement costs significantly during the next decade and that the combined effects will increase the annual rate of productivity growth by 0.25 percent over what it might be otherwise.

We are dubious that there is that much imperfect competition among supplier firms to be "corrected" by the Internet. Moreover, we believe the Goldman Sachs estimate suffers from a more fundamental conceptual flaw. Although the Internet may reduce profit margins among suppliers somewhat, any resulting reduction in prices that they charge will not directly reduce the quantity of inputs required to generate the same level of output—that is, they will not increase productivity. Instead, any cost savings from lower supplier profit margins will represent a *transfer of income* from suppliers to producers. Moreover, if the markets in which the final goods and services are sold are competitive—and this is likely to be the case for the vast majority of those markets—the benefits of reduced supplier margins will then be passed on to *consumers*. The same result should occur to the extent that the Internet also causes profit margins among final producers to fall, as it should for standardized "plain vanilla" products and services for which price is the most important factor in a purchaser's decision (such as books, common financial instruments, mortgages, and most lines of personal insurance). In short, to the extent that the Internet compresses profit margins throughout the economy, the benefits will show up in the form of lower prices to consumers—perhaps in a series of one-time gains—but not in added productivity.

Nonetheless, a compression of profit margins throughout the supply chain is quite likely to enhance true productivity in another fashion. With less room for error, firms should be more focused on adopting the kinds of cost-savings measures, already described, that should reduce the quantity of inputs required to generate any given level of output. Moreover, in a competitive environment, it is likely that inefficient firms will be weeded out more quickly so that at any given time there should be more firms in each market operating at cutting-edge levels of efficiency. Furthermore, this "Schumpeterian" process of creative destruction should free up resources formerly used in inefficient firms and tasks for more productive activities elsewhere in the economy. To be sure, the transitions for the individuals involved can be difficult and painful, as can any innovations that affect people's livelihoods.

These effects should raise the average level of productivity in each sector and, in turn, the entire economy. Our sector studies, however, have not attempted to isolate these types of effects—indeed, it is not clear that such impacts can be quantified—and for this reason (among others) the total quantifiable estimates of the Internet on productivity presented later may well be conservative.

Where the Benefits Show Up

Some Internet effects clearly contribute to productivity but will not show up primarily in the productivity statistics of the sectors in which the gains are generated. In their paper on the trucking industry, the University of Michigan research team demonstrates how modern logistics firms, hooked up by the Internet to fleets of trucks, help manage increasingly complex order delivery patterns for their business customers, combining all means of transportation (truck, rail, and air) to produce the most efficient means of moving goods among various locations. Because the logistics firms have fundamentally altered the nature of the services they offer, the savings they generate do not primarily show up in the transportation sector. Instead, the improved transportation management reduces costs incurred by the customers themselves—perhaps by as much as $71 billion on an annual basis within the next five years, as discussed later. These savings *will* show up in the GDP statistics in lower costs for the many sectors that *use* transportation services (so-called downstream sectors) and thus will add to productivity growth as they materialize.

Similarly, the additional choice and convenience afforded by the Internet may generate cost savings in other ways that also find their way into the official output data. The Dell model, which allows customers to pick the characteristics they want in a product and then have the customized product shipped directly to them from the factory, may eventually reduce distribution costs for automobiles and other big-ticket items. This "build-to-order" process would reduce the need for extensive inventories by manufacturers and dealers (cost savings that would be reflected in the productivity data), while saving shopping time for the consumers who insist on specific features of the product they purchase (benefits that probably would not be counted).

Likewise, as noted above, productivity improvements that result from more intensive use of the Internet in interactions between government and business will show up partly in lowering the cost of government itself and partly in reducing the costs to businesses of paying taxes, obtaining permits, and the like. Productivity growth in health care may also manifest itself in lower business costs.

Adding It All Up

The evidence from the sector studies, when cumulated, leads to the following broad conclusions:

—The *potential* of the Internet to enhance productivity growth over the next few years is real.

—Much of the impact of the Internet may not be felt in e-commerce per se, but in lower costs for quite mundane transactions that involve information flows—ordering, invoicing, filing claims, and making payments—across a wide range of old economy sectors, including health care and government.

—The Internet produces considerable scope for management efficiencies in product development, supply chain management, and a variety of other aspects of business performance.

—The Internet will enhance competition, both increasing efficiency and reducing profit margins throughout the economy, but the profit squeeze itself should not be counted as a productivity enhancement.

—The Internet is likely to yield some cost reductions that show up as productivity gains in industries or sectors other than those in which the savings may be initially generated.

But can these projected productivity gains be quantified at least roughly? How significant are they likely to be? Table 3-1 tabulates the projected cost savings that the authors of each of the sector studies have estimated. All estimates refer to the potential annual cost reductions that the sector experts believe to be achievable within the next five years.

Table 3-1. *Estimates of Potential Internet-Related Cost Savings*
Billions of 2000 dollars

Sector	Annual cost savings in five years
Education	Not clear
Financial services	19
Government	At least 12
Health care	41
Manufacturing	50–100
Retailing	Not clear
Trucking	3–79
Total	125–251

In sum, table 3-1 suggests that the total cost savings for sectors that collectively account for about 70 percent of GDP fall roughly between $125 billion and $251 billion. In an economy with annual output today of roughly $10 trillion (in 2000 dollars), these savings represent 1.25 to 2.5 percent of current GDP (a bit smaller share of GDP five years hence). This range reflects the cumulative savings of primarily one-time cost reductions. In reality, the savings are likely to accrue over time, as cutting-edge techniques spread from first movers to later adopters. Over the five-year period, therefore, the foregoing total savings estimates imply annualized gains in productivity—relative to a baseline in which the Internet is not present—of about 0.25 to 0.5 percent.

Several points about what the table does and does not include should be kept in mind. First, the Internet is not projected to generate measured cost savings in all of the sectors. Education and retailing, in particular, stand out as exceptions to the general pattern. This is not because the experts on these sectors expect the Internet to have no impact. To the contrary, as Austin Goolsbee documents, the Internet is expected to make it easier for many students to take advantage of distance learning, as it already has at a number of colleges and business schools and within corporations (especially for the teaching of IT-related subjects). Similarly, Joseph Bailey demonstrates how e-tailing has enhanced customer convenience while compressing profit margins of all retailers, thus lowering prices. Furthermore, even in those sectors where the Internet is projected to have a significant *absolute* impact—measured in total dollar cost savings—because the sectors themselves are so large (manufacturing, for example), the impact will still remain small in *percentage* terms.

Second, table 3-1 subsumes within the manufacturing cost saving figure the cost-reducing impact of the Internet in one particular subsector—automobile manufacturing and sales. Based on what they believe to be the most reliable reports from Wall Street analysts, Charles Fine and Dan Raff estimate that the Internet could shave as much as 13 percent of the cost of producing the average automobile. Like the estimates for the other sectors, Fine and Raff believe these savings are likely to be realized in "one shot" rather than in continued improvements. Even so, as long as they do not occur all at the same time in all firms, the cumulative effect of these one-time improvements should improve measured productivity growth in the automobile industry during the period of adjustment.

Third, the estimates for some of the sectors are expressed in ranges rather than point estimates, and in some cases—notably, for the trucking industry—that range is rather wide, reflecting the considerable uncertainty about the Internet's likely economic impact. For example, the savings estimates for the manufacturing sector are based on the assumption that firms within the sector, on average, are less successful than industry leader Cisco has been in using the Internet to cut production costs. Even so, the range for savings estimates reported in the table reflects considerable conservatism about other firms' relative success; the upper-bound figure, for example, assumes that the average firm is able to reduce its costs by just 2 percent, well below the 5 percent cost reduction estimated by Cisco. Meanwhile, a major reason for the large range in the case of trucking is that the lion's share of the estimated cost savings is in sectors that *use* trucking services rather than in trucking itself. Given the diversity of customers and the industries in which they compete, this provides another complication that is not present in the case of the other sector studies.

Fourth, table 3-1 does not include estimates of the investment spending that may be required to generate the cost savings. In fact, there is some evidence that companies need only spend relatively small sums for software and added hardware to make their business operations more Internet ready. Most of the required spending is for personnel who must reengineer the companies' internal processes. Such spending for what MIT economist Erik Brynjolfsson has called "organizational capital" is expensed and consists of a reallocation of employees that firms already have on board plus perhaps some fees for consultants. In any event, a fully accurate accounting for the impact of the Internet on productivity should take account of the additional expenditures for both physical and human capital that are required to generate the savings just summarized. It could be that we are too optimistic about the investment required; after all, one rule of thumb in the computer industry is that IT projects cost twice as much and take twice as long to complete as one thinks at the outset.

However large the productivity savings turn out to be—and the accumulated preliminary estimates reported here suggest the annual economywide cost savings, once fully realized, could exceed $200 billion annually—there should be no mistake about who the ultimate beneficiaries will be: consumers, not businesses. In our highly and increasingly competitive market, most temporary market advantages—reflected in high profit margins—get competed away (unless firms accumulate and then abuse their monopoly positions). Perhaps the best evidence for this is that relative shares of national income going to labor, on the one hand, and capital (interest payments, dividends, and retained profits), on the other, have been remarkably stable for several decades. Why then will firms invest and make increasing use of the Internet if they cannot permanently enjoy the extra profits? Very simply, because they will have no other choice. If they do not stay at the cutting edge, then someone else will. Andrew Grove of Intel could not have put it any better than in his famous book title *Only the Paranoid Survive*.

The productivity gains from the Internet will not necessarily increase the already high productivity growth rate of the past few years. All we have attempted to do in this project is to isolate the portion of any future productivity growth that may reasonably be attributed to the Internet, or more precisely, to networked communications (which would also include intranets). The actual productivity growth rate will be some combination of Internet-specific contributions plus the continued contribution of other technologies, improvements in workplace practices, and capital deepening—the same processes that have contributed to productivity growth in the past.

Finally, the estimates produced for this project more or less assume the continuing use and penetration of existing Internet-related technologies, including the extended rollout of broadband as a vehicle for transmitting data to and from individual users, whose more extensive use of the Internet could then put more competitive pressure on many firms (more on this in chapter 5). More important, it is entirely possible that within the next five or ten years, another disruptive technological advance associated with the Internet—fiber optic cable connected to many, if not most, businesses and homes—could be just as transformative in its impacts as the current Internet is projected to be. Should this be the case, then our estimates understate the ultimate impact of the Internet. At the other extreme, it is possible that the nightmare scenario envisioned by some experts—a major hacker attack by terrorists or other criminals that brings the entire Internet down for some time—unfolds, thereby not only severely disrupting commerce and perhaps financial markets, but over the longer run causing a loss of confidence in the security and reliability of the Internet. Should this dark scenario come to life, then our estimates may prove to be too optimistic.

4 *Benefits of the Internet That May Not Show Up in the GDP*

MOST OF THIS BOOK focuses attention on one particular effect of the Internet—its impact on the productivity of the economy. Productivity, as we have seen, is extremely important to our standard of living. If use of the Internet makes productivity grow faster, we will all be able to live better without working any harder. To the extent that the Internet increases productivity, that increase will show up in higher output of goods and services, measured—however imperfectly—by the gross domestic product. Beyond its impact on productivity, however, the Internet will have myriad other effects on how the economy works, what people buy and sell, and how they spend their time. These effects may not have a measurable dollar value and are unlikely to be fully or even partially reflected in the GDP.

To say something has no dollar value is not to say it is worthless. On the contrary, some of the attributes of our society that citizens value most highly are ones on which they cannot put a price tag. Citizens cherish fundamental rights—the right to vote, to speak freely, to be represented by counsel if they are accused of a crime—natural beauty and the continued existence of wild places, freedom from fear of war and crime and disease. Indeed, Americans often call these attributes "priceless" to indicate how highly they are valued.

This chapter discusses briefly some the benefits of the Internet that may not have price tags but that are nevertheless valuable: increased convenience; a wider range of choices; reduction of errors that may save pain and even lives; and increased ability to work from home, to express political opinions, and to interact with like-minded individuals in distant places. Some of the most enthusiastic supporters of the Internet regard these hard-to-measure benefits as more important than the estimated productivity gains reported in the previous chapter. Some nonquantifiable impacts have downsides, however, and different people may value these impacts very differently. Some benefits, such as working from home, may have major effects that spill over onto others not directly involved in the Internet activity in question.

Convenience

Anyone who has shopped on the web (and we suspect almost all of the readers of this book have done so at least occasionally) realizes that a major advantage of such shopping is convenience—both convenience of time and convenience of place. One can sit at one's own computer at any time of the day or night and order all manner of goods and services with the click of a mouse, without driving or walking to a store, branch bank, or other business location. Some people are already shopping by punching buttons on a cell phone, and many more are expected to do so in the years ahead. The added convenience of being able to obtain information, to search for the "best" or most suitable product, and to complete transactions on line is a real benefit for many consumers. The use of the Internet for distance learning can save travel time for both teachers and students and permit flexibility in scheduling that may benefit both. Similarly, working at home via the Internet ("telecommuting") offers two kinds of convenience to workers: It saves them the time and money that would otherwise be spent in commuting to and from the workplace, which may be considerable; and it often allows them a more flexible work schedule that fits better with their family and other responsibilities than a regular nine-to-five job.

It is not easy to put a price tag on convenience. A product bought on line and delivered to the door is effectively a higher-quality product than one that must be searched out in a store and carried home by the buyer. Some customers are willing to pay a higher price for the convenience of shopping on the net. Consider, for example, the Amazon.com customer who is willing to pay more for a book, once the cost of delivery is factored in, than for the same book at a local bookshop. This customer is demonstrating through a willingness to pay extra that convenience is worth something to her.

The government statisticians who track prices of goods in order to provide estimates of inflation make serious efforts to adjust for improvements in product quality, including the added

convenience that may be associated with Internet-based purchasing. In practice, however, it is difficult for them to find ways
to do so. One approach to isolating the benefits of Internet convenience is to compare the prices (net of any taxes) of the same
product purchased online and off and then to attribute any difference to the benefits of convenience. This may be reasonable if
the delivered price of the online product is higher. But greater
price transparency, more competition, or other factors may make
the product bought on line *cheaper* than its offline counterpart.
In that event the price comparison approach for measuring the
benefits of convenience does not work.

Another approach to measuring the benefits of convenience is
to compute the average monetary value of the time savings
involved in buying something on the net relative to the time
required to travel to a store, search for the product, wait in line to
purchase it, and then travel back home. One can make plausible
assumptions about the time involved in these activities and calcu-
late the total value of that time based on the customer's wage rate,
for example. This method implies that the convenience of shopping on the net is worth more to people who earn higher wages
than to those who earn lower ones, because high-wage earners
give up more pay when they take time away from their jobs.

It is likely that people at the upper end of the wage scale, on
the average, put a relatively high monetary value on time-saving
conveniences, including use of the Internet. It is hard to know for
certain whether they do, however, because people with more
income can afford to spend more on everything. They are more
likely to have computers and access to the net. They are on the
right side of the digital divide.

Other individual differences come into play as well. Some people, perhaps especially teenage girls, actually enjoy shopping. They like to spend time in stores or malls searching for the "right" color, style, fit, or price and consulting with their friends. For them, shopping is an amusing leisure activity that does not compete with time spent at work. Other people hate shopping and regard it as a necessary chore, only a step above visiting the dentist. Most of us are probably somewhere in between—we find some shopping fun and some a necessary, but tedious, activity. It is not clear how enjoyment of shopping correlates with wages or anything else. To the extent that people like to shop, valuing the time saved by Internet shopping at the average wage will overstate the value of online shopping convenience. This calculation hardly seems a useful exercise until a lot more is known about attitudes toward different modes of acquiring goods.

In any event, however it may be measured in principle, in reality convenience afforded by the net does not now show up in the GDP data as a form of additional output, nor is it likely to in the future. Convenience therefore will not be included as a social benefit by the official statisticians who add up the productivity benefits of the net.

More Choices

The greater range of choice that consumers and business purchasers have in an e-marketplace stems partly from the ability of the net to bring distant and hard-to-find suppliers into the same market, thus broadening the choices available to buyers. If the product is a standardized one, such as a brand-name refrigerator or a thirty-year home mortgage, the benefit to the buyer of access to the broader and more transparent e-marketplace may take the form of a lower price. If the product is unique or extremely specialized—say, a rare book or an unusual piece of antique furniture—the benefit to the consumer of reducing the cost of search may simply be in finding the desired item at all.

A related and often lauded characteristic of the Internet is that it facilitates customization: it gives consumers an easy way to order and receive goods and services tailored to their needs and preferences. For example, the computer on which part of this book was written, a Dell, was ordered with various customized features over the Internet. To be sure, the same thing might have been accomplished had one of us gone to a store and purchased another personal computer (Dell only sells direct, over the telephone or the Internet). But it would have been far more time consuming to do so, and there is no guarantee that the store would have in stock precisely the configuration that one of us wanted—and got—by filling out a brief order form on the net.

Another related benefit of the Internet arises from new products and services that the communication medium has made and will make possible. The evolution of Napster, discussed in more detail in the next chapter, is a prime example. As any reader of this book (or at least his or her children) will know, Napster became an almost overnight sensation by allowing individuals to download sound recordings from other computers by establishing a central directory of available recordings from all participating members. The service was eventually shut down by the courts as facilitating copyright violations, but new similar services that do not rely on a central directory—and that are less obviously unlawful and unstoppable in any event—have sprung up in its place. This kind of service would have been impossible without the Internet. Whether you regard the service as good or bad (certainly most of the music industry thinks this is bad), it is a service that would have been unthinkable without the net. Expect more as yet unimagined, preferably lawful, services in the future.

The benefits of more choice and customization are difficult to quantify and even more difficult to value. In principle, surveys can ask consumers to place a value on being able to choose from among ten different styles of shirts or pants (as opposed to one or two), but the weakness of all surveys is that they do not reflect actual transaction prices. Some consumers may be willing to pay more for a suit in a store offering a wide selection than the identical suit sold in a location with far fewer offerings, because the ability to choose from a broad menu on the spot saves one or more additional trips to other stores. But one cannot simply assume that the higher price at the store with wider selection (if, indeed, the price is higher, which may not even be the case) embodies the value of wider choice. It may reflect other unrelated differences in costs. In short, there is no easy way to use either survey or transactions data to compute the value of wider choice.

None of this is to deny that, in principle, the Internet almost surely provides many consumers with benefits of broader choice. It is just difficult in practice to quantify the value of those benefits.

Reducing Errors, Saving Lives

Another important source of Internet benefits that are not counted in the official statistics is the reduction of costly mistakes. More accurate, faster, and cheaper information flow, facilitated by the Internet, may be expected to reduce may kinds of errors—financial, engineering, and law enforcement errors, for example. But perhaps the most dramatic possibilities lie in the Internet's potential for reducing medical mistakes.

As it is now, needless injuries and deaths result from the current fragmented way in which patient records are maintained and coordinated and information about best practices is disseminated.[1] Some of the problem is attributable to simple mistakes that arise when nurses and pharmacies cannot read a physician's handwritten notes. The Internet and related computer technology should reduce at least part of this problem, assuming that security and authentication issues can be resolved. In the process technology will save lives and produce better medical outcomes for patients who otherwise would have been victims of these mistakes. Errors arising from illegible handwriting would be eliminated if hospital physicians learned to use handheld computers to record their observations of patients and to order prescriptions, through built-in wireless connections, directly from pharmacies.

Even more important, the Internet should enable physicians to reduce diagnostic errors by being able to pull up patients' complete medical histories from a central database at any point in the treatment process.[2] The Internet will greatly facilitate the transfer of medical records among providers, from doctor's office to clinic to hospital, thus improving the quality of care and reducing errors arising from one provider's ignorance of what another has already done or prescribed.

At least three challenges stand in the way of realizing this new medical world of instant and more accurate communications, however. One is the development and adoption of standardized record formats for medical records. The second is the development of widely acceptable privacy rules and the data security measures needed to make sure the rules cannot easily be broken. The third, and perhaps most challenging, involves changing the culture of medical practitioners (which may be even more difficult than changing the internal workings of many corporations).

Many older doctors now practicing are not likely to embrace computer technology easily or readily. To be sure, hospitals may be able to address this problem by having nurses or physician's assistants record relevant information in digital form, but this process would add to the cost of the technology and thus reduce or eliminate any productivity benefits while also retaining some source of error in transcription. Moreover, even if doctors or their assistants become comfortable with the technology, the software, some of which already exists, must be refined and standardized so that all professionals in the medical chain are speaking the same digital "language." In short, a process of diffusion will be required to produce substantial lifesaving benefits, and the speed at which these benefits are realized depends on how rapidly bureaucratic inertia and personal habits can be overcome. Slow diffusion and cultural resistance to change are, of course, challenges in all industries and sectors, not just in medicine.

The reduction of errors in transmitting medical information is only one way in which Internet technology can be used to save lives. From the earliest days of the Internet, some enthusiasts have touted "telemedicine" as the next "big thing" that might transform the medical industry and treatment of patients. A patient sitting in an isolated town in North Dakota can be diagnosed (and perhaps one day even be treated) by highly specialized doctors sitting in their offices in such world-famous medical facilities as the Mayo Clinic in Rochester, Minnesota, or the Johns Hopkins University Hospital in Baltimore.

However, several practical considerations impede the widespread use of telemedicine. Highly specialized, cutting-edge physicians have only limited time to devote to multiple patients. Indeed, the same is true of all physicians. Some doctors use e-mail to communicate with their patients, but most of those who are comfortable with computers do not take advantage of the technology to interact with patients. Their time is limited, and their compensation is based on office visits, not e-mail responses. Furthermore, state licensing laws restrict the ability of out-of-state doctors to provide medical advice from distant locations. A patient can lawfully travel to a doctor out of state, of course, but may not be able to take advice directly from the same physician over the Internet (or even the telephone, for that matter) unless the distant physician has a license to practice medicine in the patient's state of residence.

The Internet nonetheless has empowered consumers everywhere by giving them much greater access than ever before to medical information. The latest research and technical information is available online from the National Institutes of Health and other leading research organizations, and more consumer-friendly types of information can be found on commercial websites (aiming to earn money with revenues from advertising and referrals) and bulletin boards maintained by individuals with similar symptoms or diseases. Easier access to medical information is a two-edged sword, however. In the hands of otherwise ill-informed consumers, medical information can lead individuals to take measures or to ingest food supplements that may not be medically appropriate and could complicate the consumer's medical condition. But enhanced information can also encourage consumers to seek treatment from trained professionals when they might not otherwise do so or to seek a second opinion when they believe their treatment is inappropriate. It is too early to know whether the benefits of the information outweigh any dangers, but as more consumers become familiar with both the Internet and their own medical conditions, we suspect the net effect (pun intended) on the health status of all users will be increasingly positive.

Suppose that the Internet really will save lives and reduce needless suffering by patients who will be more quickly and accurately diagnosed and treated. This would be a significant benefit to society. But will it show up as added output for the economy? The short answer is probably not. There is no market in which individuals buy and sell quality of life or its longevity—the outputs, one might say, of medical services. What enters the GDP instead are the *inputs* into that process, such as expenditures on medical care and pharmaceuticals. Statisticians make an effort to measure improvements in the efficiency with which those inputs are used to produce health outcomes. As we discussed in the last chapter, the Internet can help produce those efficiencies by reducing the heavy volume of paperwork now required to process claims and pay providers. But measured GDP does not go up simply because the Internet may allow more people to live longer and better lives as a result of their physicians' (or their own) use of the Internet. That is because the GDP, as it is now, does not measure the value of life or its quality—concepts that are hard to define and even more difficult to measure in practice.

By whatever means they occur, improvements in the effectiveness of medical care for the working-age population are likely to increase both hours worked and the productivity of those hours by reducing days lost to illness. It is not so clear that improvements in the effectiveness of medical care for older people actually raise measured output. Whether enhancing longevity will contribute to higher measured output depends on whether those who are living longer continue to be healthy, energetic, and both able and willing to stay in the work force at older ages, at least part of the time. If large numbers of older people work longer into what are now considered retirement ages, measured output will go up, although not necessarily output per hour worked.

The bottom line, however, is that most Americans will doubtless welcome whatever contribution the Internet can make to improving the effectiveness of medical care and reducing illness and death regardless of the impact on measured GDP. This provides another stark illustration that money isn't everything in the world, and thus the impact of the Internet on what people value most is not necessarily fully or even adequately captured by the productivity estimates reported in the last chapter.

Working at Home and Telecommuting

Many other ways that the Internet is being used now and will be used in the future may have important effects on how Americans live and work, effects that may not show up in measured GDP. One obvious impact of the Internet has been on the extent to which workers are able to work from home. Millions of Americans now work primarily or exclusively from home, and this trend may accelerate if fear of terrorism becomes a permanent feature of American life. Some of these people are running their own businesses out of their homes, consulting or producing goods and services marketed primarily on the net. Some of them are telecommuting, in the sense that they are still interacting with an office or other workplace over the Internet but avoiding a physical journey to work at least part of the time.

The effects telecommuting may have on hours worked or the productivity of employees are not yet clear. On the one hand, telecommuting probably allows many more people to join the labor force or to continue working. This raises overall economic output, although not necessarily productivity. Some workers who would be in the labor force in any event may find their productivity enhanced by fewer interruptions and reduced stress. They may find they work better on their own schedules, at times when their productivity may be highest. Or they may produce more simply because they are not tired out by a long, aggravating drive to work. On the other hand, some telecommuters may find their productivity diminished because, by working at home, they lose valuable interactions with supervisors and coworkers. Possible negative impacts are likely to be reduced by the fact that most individuals who telecommute presumably do so by choice. If they find that they are not as productive or that their likelihood of promotion is diminished in the process, many are likely to return to their offices. On balance, we suspect that to the extent that the Internet enables more telecommuting, it is adding to economic output, although the impact on productivity is uncertain.

If working from home and telecommuting begins to affect a large portion of the labor force, the result could be to reduce the concentration of employment and ease traffic congestion along normal commuting routes considerably. The Internet is already enabling some people to move their businesses to places where they find the surroundings beautiful and the quality of life high. In addition, even if workers do not produce more by telecommuting, they certainly place some value on the time they are not waiting in traffic (although this benefit will not show up in the official output statistics). In addition, any reduction in traffic congestion should improve productivity by making transportation more efficient. It remains to be seen how strong any or all of these trends become.

Social Networks, Politics, and Democracy

There are widely divergent opinions about how use of the Internet affects social interaction. Some observers view the use of computers, especially the large blocks of time many people spend surfing the net, as contributing to the breakdown of social interaction. They worry that young people and adults are spending hours on the Internet that would otherwise be spent in group activities involving family, neighbors, schoolmates, or coworkers.[3]

In contrast, a widely discussed *benefit* of the Internet is that it is providing new "social" benefits by assisting in the creation of new cyber-communities.[4] Unlike their physical counterparts, these cyber- or virtual communities are defined not by geographic proximity but by interest. Chat rooms are now available for seemingly anyone and anything. Many individuals somehow feel freer and more able to communicate when writing e-mails and notes to bulletin boards than when speaking directly to other individuals. People with life-threatening illnesses have found new support groups on the net. Among the most enthusiastic users of the new technology are academic scholars, many of whom use the Internet daily to communicate with other experts in their fields, as well as to collaborate on articles or books in a fashion and at a speed that only a short time ago would have been unimaginable.[5] We believe all of these social benefits of the Internet are very real and, on balance, are likely to be welfare-improving, although none is likely ever to show up in measured GDP.

A related social effect of the Internet grows out of its global character, and specifically the fact that it has facilitated political organizational activity that has crossed national borders. While there certainly can be value to greater communication, not all cross-border communication necessarily enhances economic welfare. We refer here to the ironic global use of the Internet to oppose the process of globalization itself.

For example, e-mail facilitated the organized opposition to the Multilateral Agreement on Investment (MAI), a proposal by countries belonging to the Organization for Economic Cooperation and Development (OECD) to relax restrictions on cross-border investment. The opposition from environmental and labor organizations in various developed countries was so intense that OECD member governments were forced to withdraw the proposal. Although the MAI had its flaws (specifically, its seemingly open invitation to lawsuits for any sort of "taking" of property), it nonetheless would have further relaxed barriers to long-term investments across borders; such investments for the most part enhance the welfare of both recipient and donor countries.

The better-known, and more recent, example of an e-mail-organized protest against globalization occurred in Seattle at the December 1999 ministerial meeting of the World Trade Organization, a meeting aimed at setting the next agenda for multilateral trade negotiations. Marches and sporadic violence disrupted the meetings and drew worldwide attention. Indeed, the protesters claimed credit for the failure of the ministerial meeting itself, although, in fact, governments had not formed a sufficient consensus on the outcome before the meeting to have guaranteed a positive result. Nonetheless, the protests galvanized opposition to further trade liberalization, and this opposition remains in both the United States and in other (mostly developed) countries today, despite overwhelming evidence that lower trade barriers would lower prices and help make consumers better off throughout the world.[6] In short, while the Internet has made it possible for so many people in so many different places throughout the globe to organize quickly and effectively to voice their views and to plan joint political activity, the MAI and Seattle experiences indicate that the greater democracy unleashed by the Internet may not always be a force for good (although the protesters may certainly think so).

The same could well be true for the increased use of the Internet here in the United States, not just for voting but also for amassing signatures so that petitions of various sorts can be more easily placed on state and local ballots. Two major impediments to this wave of e-democracy are ensuring security and addressing complaints that Internet voting violates the equal protection guarantee written into the Fourteenth Amendment to the Constitution (because access to the Internet differs by income and racial group). It is possible, although by no means certain, that both of these problems will be overcome, the first by technology and the second through the establishment of Internet terminals in many places of public access (post offices, libraries, schools) so that even those individuals without access at home can gain easy access to the net through a public facility.

It is far from clear, however, that even if the obstacles are removed, using the Internet to vote and, in particular, to put initiatives on ballots necessarily would be a positive development, on balance. On the one hand, Internet voting could help improve the precision with which votes are counted, thus avoiding a repeat of the events of the 2001 presidential election that culminated in the still hotly debated Supreme Court ruling in favor of George Bush. More precision in vote counting would be an unambiguous positive development. On the other hand, scholars and journalists are likely to argue for some time whether the increase in direct democracy that the Internet may generate should be viewed in the same favorable light.

Voter-driven initiatives may well be democratic, but too much democracy is not necessarily a good thing. The prospect that the Internet may soon allow individuals to click their positions on various issues of the day is not consistent with how our democracy is supposed to work. Our political system is a *representative* democracy, one that relies on political leaders elected by the people to make choices on tough issues. Elections are held for the purpose of choosing the agents to whom we delegate this power, not for the purpose of having individuals make important public decisions themselves. A system of cyber-voting coupled with electronically enabled ballot initiatives could easily degenerate into a "knee-jerk" democracy dominated by the whims and emotions of the electorate at particular points in time, with results that can hardly be guaranteed always to be positive.

For now, however, such worst-case outcomes are speculative at best. So far, the Internet appears to have promoted citizen participation in public life at many levels—local, national, and international—and thereby has helped reduce citizen alienation from what can often seem like abstract and distant decisionmaking processes. But improvements in process do not guarantee better outcomes. No doubt, some years will have to pass before anyone knows whether the Internet will help or harm the American political system and in the process improve or detract from overall economic performance.

5 *Realizing the Internet's Potential*

WHAT WILL DETERMINE the extent to which the potential benefits of the Internet—both the quantifiable improvements to productivity and the less quantifiable benefits of convenience and quality improvement—will, in fact, materialize, and at what pace? In estimating the future impact of Internet use on productivity growth (see chapter 3), we implicitly assumed that firms would follow a more or less continuous path of improvement in introducing Internet-related technologies and adapting their business practices to them. The reality, of course, may well be different.

A wide variety of factors will affect the rate at which the benefits from the Internet will be realized. One way to think about the pace of change is to distinguish among three types of benefits:

—those that are likely to grow out of the increased penetration of the Internet throughout the currently unconnected population (the "width" of the Internet revolution);

—those that may arise from more intensive use of and adaptation to the Internet (its "depth"); and

—those that are likely to come from the build-out of a faster Internet or the penetration of broadband (its "speed").

Each of these channels of influence will be affected by public policies relating to the Internet. Mindful of the large uncertainties surrounding these topics, we nonetheless offer some views on each of them.

Internet Penetration

Clearly, the more rapidly individuals and firms gain access to the Internet, the faster the pace at which its benefits can be realized. At this writing, about half of all Americans own personal computers, and most of them have access to the Internet; roughly 40 percent of households are connected. We have not seen a breakdown for commercial users of the Internet, but it is safe to assume that all large businesses have Internet access, most likely at speeds considerably faster than those available to individuals at home, and many small businesses have access as well. The same is true of nonprofit and governmental organizations.

The prospects for further penetration of the Internet lie predominantly in expanding household use by bridging the digital divide that runs primarily along income lines and consequently has a differential impact on racial and ethnic minorities with low incomes.[1] The digital divide is a new manifestation of a long-standing problem: the gulf between people with skills, education, and opportunities to earn good wages, on one side, and those with limited skills, little education, and low earning capacity, on the other. The personal computer and connections to the Internet have become new symbols of the gap between the advantaged and the disadvantaged, but they also hold out great promise of helping to bridge that gap.

States and the federal government, with the cooperation of cable networks and technology companies, have made strenuous efforts to ensure that all of the nation's schools, including schools in low-income communities, have classroom computers and access to the Internet. This effort has been successful in bringing more than 75 percent of schools on line.[2] Currently, the greatest needs are for more effective teacher training to ensure that the new tools are used effectively in the classroom and the development of new curricula and classroom materials that can help teachers make maximum use of the vast educational resources available on the net. If used effectively in schools, the Internet has the potential not only of helping to bridge the digital divide, but of reducing the isolation of communities in remote rural areas and culturally insular inner-city neighborhoods.

If efforts to bridge the digital divide are focused exclusively on the young, however, the divide will narrow very slowly. Many schools are making their computer labs available for parent and other adult learning in the evenings and on weekends. Community centers in public housing projects and other low-income areas are beginning to offer computer instruction and Internet access to adults and to young people in after-school programs. More resources and effort along these lines, combined with literacy and other basic skills training, could turn the digital divide into a digital bridge across income and cultural barriers.

Fortunately, one of the outstanding features of the computer and telecommunications revolution is the steep decline in the price of the necessary equipment. As tools to access the Internet, including cellular phones and personal computers, become cheaper, the divide will gradually close. As it does, nonquantifiable benefits such as convenience will surely rise. In addition, the more pervasive e-commerce becomes, the greater will be the pressure on firms to adopt cutting-edge cost-saving techniques that can be passed on to consumers and improve their standard of living.

Use of the Internet

Although increasing access to the net is important to realizing its potential, more intensive *use* of the net by those who have access is even more important. As we outlined in earlier chapters, the largest potential economic gains from the Internet lie in its use by business, and the business sector is still in the early stages of using the Internet to cut costs and improve service. One of the participants in our larger study, Andrew McAfee, has described it this way: "Whenever I visit software companies, I get them to complete the sentence: 'The business-to-business revolution is x%

complete.' The biggest number I have heard is 5 percent. Many say 1 percent."[3]

How rapidly this revolution proceeds from that very low base will depend heavily on changes in organizational culture. Investments in capital equipment are not a key constraint. Large businesses and most smaller businesses already have computers and fast telephone connections. To "web-enable" the firm, managers do not need more equipment, but instead require a relatively modest investment in designing web pages and acquiring software to routinize communications with suppliers and customers for taking orders, tracking inventory, ordering supplies, and so on. By far the largest and most challenging investment, however, is in "organizational capital"—the time devoted to training and reorganizing the way employees carry out their jobs.

If past experience with information technology investments is any guide, successful investment in organizational capital takes enormous skill. The business and government landscapes are littered with examples of poorly planned IT projects that floundered, not because the hardware or software did not work when used properly, but because training and organizational adaptation to the new systems were inadequate. It takes time and effort to change business processes, not just to iron out software bugs, but to get people and organizations to change the way they do their jobs. Implementing change while shedding workers, which is the way the Internet generates productivity gains, can be especially difficult. It is not surprising, therefore, that in a recent issue of one of the economics profession's foremost journals, the *Journal of Economic Perspectives*, two of the leading scholars of the high-tech sector conclude that changes in manufacturing processes, in particular, on account of the Internet are likely to proceed "relatively slowly."[4] By similar reasoning, one could be pessimistic, or at least very cautious, about the pace of change in other sectors as well.

Positive change could come about more quickly, however. Provided that the antitrust laws are fully enforced (a subject we take up shortly), competition should supply a positive countervailing force to bureaucratic inertia or active resistance. Firms that are realizing the benefits from the Internet will gain market share at the expense of those who are not and thereby encourage others to move rapidly to integrate the Internet into their business processes. When companies like General Electric advertise to the world that they plan to reshape all of their business lines to be web-enabled, from ordering supplies to dealing with customers, they send a powerful message to the rest of corporate America.[5] Perhaps Oracle's advertising claims that its own business software saved the company $1 billion in costs are overstated, but the company's ad at least has caught the attention of corporate managers throughout the economy.

It is even possible that the negative business conditions at the end of 2001 (when we finished writing this book) will accelerate change by intensifying pressures on companies to cut costs in order to maintain profitability or at least to keep declines in profits to a minimum. To be sure, some firms will respond to the slowdown by curtailing plans for changing their business methods, fearing disruption to their organizations and employee morale. But we suspect many other firms will have the opposite reaction, realizing that necessity is the mother of invention and that there is no better time to introduce radical change than when revenue growth slows or turns negative and improving productivity is the only way to increase profitability.[6]

Finally, because both trade and the Internet are increasingly global phenomenons, benefits of the net for firms in any particular country are not likely to be fully realized until and unless firms abroad also make use of the Internet to change their business operations. For example, making e-commerce work well requires that both the buyer and the seller are exchanging information via the net. If one of the parties is overseas, then the party here at home cannot realize the net's full potential until its foreign counterparties have joined the system. In this sense, network externalities are not fully realized unless the network is global. The pace of change abroad, therefore, will influence the pace of productivity improvement here at home.

Speed of the Internet

The estimates of benefits from the Internet presented in earlier chapters rest on an implicit assumption: that the configuration of the Internet more or less remains as it is and that the significant changes lie in the speed with which it is adopted by businesses to cut costs. But the Internet itself is becoming faster, or more precisely, the infrastructure of the net is allowing ever more rapid communications of larger quantities of data. This is what the "bandwidth" revolution is all about. The higher the bandwidth of a communication network, the more data it can carry and at faster speeds. Although Marshall McLuhan was referring to television when he suggested that the "medium is the message," he could have just as well been talking about the Internet. More bandwidth means not just faster content delivery, but different content. If you are using a 56 kilobit modem, you are unlikely to be downloading many movies, which have too much information to squeeze through the relatively narrow copper wire "pipes" that lead into your house (and your computer) in a relatively short period of time. But once you get "broadband"—souped-up copper wires through Asynchronous Digital Subscriber Lines (DSL, for short), coaxial cable television lines, or perhaps satellite services that each can deliver information at speeds of one megabit a second or more—you have the power to download movies in a half hour or less. Suddenly, what once seemed remote now becomes possible (assuming that technology can prevent the pirating of movies and other types of content, a subject discussed later).

In short, the infrastructure of the Internet determines the content that can and will be transmitted over it. To borrow from the much overused, but still instructive, analogy to highways, not many people would want a high-powered car if they could drive only on crowded two-lane roads. But once a four- or six-lane interstate highway is opened, demand jumps for faster and more powerful cars, until that highway, too, becomes crowded. The same is true of content on the Internet.

What difference to productivity will more bandwidth make? Clearly, as more households obtain the service, Internet use per household is likely to increase, and so will e-commerce of various forms. One of the major drawbacks to existing PCs with modem connections at speeds of 56K or less is that users must "boot up" their computers and establish a new dial-in connection each time they want to access the Internet. This time-consuming process— a few minutes now matter much more to the wired population than one ever would have imagined—deters the use of the Internet for such routine, but frequent, tasks as paying bills electronically (something that only about 10 percent of American households do currently) or looking up information that may be needed quickly. With broadband, the Internet connection is always "on"; no waiting is required. With easier access to the Internet, consumers are very likely to make more intensive use of it. As this happens, the Internet should not only deliver more of those nonquantifiable gains discussed in the previous chapter, but also intensify the pressure on firms to become more efficient in delivering services and taking orders over the Internet and thus help speed the pace at which the quantifiable cost savings are actually produced.

Internet speed for businesses is a different issue. Most large businesses currently have high-speed telephone lines that are equivalent to, or even faster than, broadband to the home. The next big jump for many businesses will be direct connections to fiber optic cables, which are capable of delivering information many times faster than residential broadband. An open question is whether, and to what extent, this potentially vast increase in speed will represent a new "disruptive technology" in its own right, generating new uses for the Internet that we cannot now imagine (although we can anticipate one use—broader use of video-conferencing in lieu of travel). In that event, the estimated cost savings outlined in chapter 3 may significantly understate the potential gains from the net, as well as the pace at which they will be realized. Public policy toward broadband providers also may have an important impact on how fast the technology is made available to users, a subject we address shortly.

Of course, with all of this extra speed, both at home and on the job, as well as the continued growth in the number of users, the architecture of the Internet itself will need to be upgraded in at least two respects. First, the number of addresses will need to be expanded. Second, the software currently used by the Internet's routers will need to be modified to cope with faster connections. In principle, both of these issues are supposed to be addressed by the latest version of Internet software, IPV6, or "next generation IP." One of the advantages of IPV6 is that Internet traffic using it can also be wrapped in versions of the existing Internet protocol, IPV4, and thus can be read by computers everywhere. Nonetheless, IPV6 is not much used, and so far there has been no economic incentive for users to do so. A critical question for the future will be how IPV6 or some future and even better protocol version will come to be adopted. Unless this happens, the Internet will not be able to handle the crushing increase in data that seems destined to flow over it.[7]

Internet Security

So far we have discussed trends or developments that are likely to affect the penetration of the Internet and its benefits in incremental fashion. One set of developments, however, could sharply interrupt any of these trends: a dramatic attack or series of attacks that disable the Internet itself. We do not mean the more or less routine "hacking" of individual websites, or even the systemic "denial of service" attacks or viruses that have infected, albeit so far relatively briefly, numerous websites and users around the world. As in the physical world, these security breaches unfortunately have become part of the landscape. Firms and individuals have had to invest in Internet security software and hardware (which reduces productivity), much as individuals have had to put locks on their doors and alarm systems in their houses.

But what if the net were shut down by a massive attack on the infrastructure itself (analogous to the infamous terrorist attack on the country in September 2001)? It is well known that the addressing and routing functions of the Internet are vulnerable to malicious interference.[8] In a worst case, an attack on the Internet's infrastructure would disable its use for an extended period. In that event, not only would current usage be interrupted, but users generally could come to view the Internet as unreliable, something that could be brought down randomly, without warning. If this attitude were to become widespread, it could discourage further use of the Internet and thus stall, if not reverse, the gains we have suggested the net should make possible.

Making the Internet more secure is a challenging technological problem that will require cooperation between the public and private sectors. Government alone cannot provide the answers. Although the federal government helped launch the Internet by initially funding its construction, the net is now a complex telecommunications network that is very much in private hands. Moreover, the software that governs Internet communication—perhaps the point of the greatest security weakness—is in the private domain and will remain so. Although upgrades of that software are in the works, the next generations of the Internet are unlikely to offer ironclad protection against potentially major disruptions.

In the meantime, users are taking matters into their own hands, as they should. Alliances of firms heavily engaged in e-commerce have been formed to alert member companies to security risks and to develop best practices for insulating companies from breaches of their own security. Nonetheless, at the end of the day, if the infrastructure itself is threatened, there is nothing individual users can do other than maintain backup systems of communication—yes, telephones, fax machines, and other hardware that once looked outdated—in case the Internet proves unreliable, in much the same way that households keep flashlights and candles in case the power goes off. Any new expenditures on these backup systems would detract from the overall savings from the Internet that we otherwise project.

The Role of Policy

Clearly, government policies, both in the United States and else-where around the world, will affect Internet usage by individuals and businesses. Here we discuss policy decisions in four specific areas—privacy, regulation of broadband providers, taxation of Internet sales, and antitrust—where the outcomes are likely to affect the pace at which benefits from the Internet will be realized. We discuss these issues primarily in an American context, but recognize that many, if not all of them, will require satisfactory resolution abroad as well. We do not delve into the thorny, com-plicated issue of whether, and to what extent, each of the issues must be resolved *globally* through new multinational institutions, or through independent actions taken by individual governments. All we point out here is that the pace at which benefits from the net eventually will be realized will depend, at least to some extent, on how these policy questions are resolved, at whatever level of government is relevant—local, national, or international.

Privacy

For many people concerns about privacy and security deter use of the Internet. If more people had confidence in the security and pri-vacy of their e-transactions, e-commerce would likely grow faster, thereby increasing the benefits from its use, both directly and, more important, indirectly (by imposing greater competitive pressure on companies to use the Internet to transform their business practices). Improving the security of the net is largely a question of developing effective technological solutions, not of developing security policy. Government regulators might insist upon certain levels of encryption, in order to minimize successful disabling of the net, but such policies are not likely to be highly controversial, because all legitimate Internet users have a stake in its security. Policies to protect the privacy of information traveling on the net, by contrast, are inherently controversial because the interests of legitimate users diverge. Individuals want to protect the confidentiality of their personal information, and sellers want to exploit that information to maximize sales and profits. Hence solutions to the privacy problem require both technological improvements and policies designed to accommodate divergent interests.

Polls indicate a high degree of public concern about privacy, but it is unclear how much these concerns affect behavior. Although large majorities say they favor privacy protection when questioned by polling organizations, Internet use continues to grow rapidly. Furthermore, it is not clear that consumers remain so broadly concerned about privacy in the wake of the September 11, 2001, terrorist attacks on the United States. Privacy advocates nonetheless argue that e-commerce would be far more substantial than it is if there were greater privacy protections on the Internet. They point to a historical analogy involving credit card adoption to support their case. When general purpose credit cards were introduced in the early 1970s, users were potentially liable for fraudulent transactions or stolen cards. But in 1977 Congress shielded users from all liability for fraud and theft over $50. Thereafter, use of the cards took off, largely because consumers then had confidence in using them. By similar reasoning, it can be argued that individuals would use the Internet more frequently and more intensively if they had more confidence their privacy would not be lost in the process (at least without their permission).

Technology can help provide that confidence by offering consumers more choices about how they want any information they provide over the net to be used.[9] Still, although most Internet sites now post a privacy policy, many fewer sites give consumers a choice to opt out of having their personal information forwarded to another party.[10] On the principle that minimum legal protections can enhance consumer comfort with a new technology, stronger minimum privacy protections both on and off the net might well encourage additional e-commerce, much like the liability limit enhanced credit card usage.

In our view, such minimum standards should include three requirements:

—vendors should provide notice to users of how their personal information might be used (and if the uses change, then individuals should be renotified, although prior protections should not be withdrawn);

—vendors should provide all customers with the right to opt out of having such information forwarded to third parties, including affiliates, for marketing purposes (this would preserve legitimate and useful transfers for payments processing, fraud detection, and other such uses); and

—vendors should afford individuals the opportunity to view files maintained about them, at some reasonable cost (the use and aggregation of unidentified personal information thereby would be exempted).

These minimum standards should be supplemented with additional provisions applying to specified classes of especially sensitive information, such as personal medical records or queries and certain personal financial data (checking account transactions and credit spending information, for example). In these instances, an "opt-in" rule would apply, meaning that personal data could not be used unless the individual took an explicit action to grant permission for its use. In fact, the Department of Health and Human Services issued rules in December 2000 that generally require health care providers and insurance companies to afford an opt-in right to individuals regarding their health information, rules which the Bush administration subsequently supported and implemented.

We are reluctant, however, at this point to recommend an across-the-board opt-in requirement for all types of personal information. Information flows are the lifeblood of our modern economy. Credit cannot be properly priced unless lenders have adequate information about borrowers, some of which they probably would not obtain voluntarily from the borrowers themselves. Other types of personally identifiable information must be transmitted for checking account, credit card, and other transactions processing to be completed. Indeed there are so many ways that information flows between individuals and companies that it would be impossible to catalogue them all and, more important, to anticipate how overly restrictive protections in the name of

"privacy protection" might interrupt those flows in ways
could impose significant costs throughout the economy.

Thus, the kind of choice individuals should have, as a matter
of right, makes a big difference, because inertia works heavily in
favor of the status quo. The experience with the opt-out choice
given consumers in the financial arena (mandated by the Gramm-
Leach-Bliley Act of 1999) confirms what one would expect: relatively few (5 percent or less) actually do opt out. Conversely, one
would expect roughly the same percentage of respondents to affir-
matively opt in if given that type of choice. Where strong reasons
exist for imposing an opt-in rule, as in the case of very sensitive
information, then those reasons should trump concerns about
costs. But until there are more clearly demonstrated harms from
giving individuals an opt-out right in other situations, it seems to
us to be premature to mandate choice in the form of an opt-in
across the board.

Whatever the minimum privacy standard, it ought to be federal and preempt state rules (ideally, it would be preferable to
have one set of privacy rules internationally, but this seems too
much to ask). Otherwise, the country could end up with fifty different and perhaps inconsistent sets of state rules, imposing
potentially significant compliance costs on all vendors, but especially on e-merchants.[11] Moreover, in this as in many other legal
areas, the question arises: whose law applies, the state where the
vendor is situated or incorporated, or the state of the consumer?
If the latter, then online retailers either would have to tailor different privacy notices to different online customers (assuming

state of residence) or, more likely, have

he most protective state, which could

ntially costly across-the-board opt-in

we have just criticized.

axes

One of the attractions to consumers of making purchases on the Internet is that they effectively avoid paying sales or use taxes that they would otherwise owe if they shopped in a local store. Austan Goolsbee, of the University of Chicago, has estimated that retail Internet sales would be roughly 25 to 30 percent lower in value if consumers had to pay their home state taxes on those sales.[12]

Enthusiasts of the Internet argue that it should remain a free resource, open to everyone without taxation or regulation, and that taxing Internet sales would be a step down a dangerous path leading to government control. Brick and mortar retailers, by contrast, see untaxed Internet merchants as competitors with an unfair advantage, but so far the law is against them. Under current law, out-of-state merchants are not obligated to collect those taxes unless they have a "physical presence" in the consumers' state. The Supreme Court established the physical presence test in the context of mail-order catalogue sales on the principle that to do otherwise would excessively burden interstate commerce. Given the many thousands of jurisdictions around the country that rely on sales taxes, with different rates and exemptions, many of which change from year to year, it is understandable why the Court ruled that it truly would be burdensome to require all merchants to charge each out-of-state resident a use tax based on the resident's home jurisdiction. Internet merchants effectively represent the next generation of mail-order stores and thus are exempt, under the same legal test, from withholding use taxes.

Yet states and localities—as well as many retailers in the offline, or "real," world—understandably are worried that if Internet commerce really takes off, sales tax revenues could decline precipitously, and many local retailers could be put out of business. The concern is legitimate. It seems inequitable to treat goods sold online differently from goods sold in the physical world. This inequity will become more apparent as e-commerce grows in importance. What should be done?

Several approaches might be taken to equalize the burden of sales taxes between in-store purchases and remote sales (including Internet sales and phone or mail orders). The most straightforward, but possibly also the most legally and practically problematic, would be a federal mandate imposed on all merchants to collect use taxes on goods purchased by out-of-state consumers. Even if the courts found no violation of the due process requirements of the Constitution—not a sure thing—such a mandate would impose a considerable burden on merchants, and hence on interstate commerce, unless a software package were available to track the various sales tax regimes in different jurisdictions on a timely basis and forward the tax proceeds to the jurisdiction. Development of such software that is timely and up to date for jurisdictions should not be taken for granted, given the variety of state and local taxes and the frequency with which they change— although Hal Varian has suggested that software that is about 95 percent accurate would not be that difficult or expensive to provide.[13] If states and localities could be induced or required to harmonize their taxes (reducing the variations in base and rate), the software would be easier to develop, but the burden on merchants of collecting the tax and getting it to the right place could still be formidable.

A variation of a federal mandate would be for the federal government to approve one or more interstate compacts, under which like-minded states would agree on a common sales tax regime (same base, same rate).[14] The states in the compact could even agree to have merchants send the taxes (presumably electronically) to a central collection authority, which would act as a clearinghouse and forward the net amount due to each state treasury at the end of each accounting period.

Yet another way of "solving" the potentially mounting problem of lost sales tax proceeds from e-commerce transactions is for states and localities that now depend on sales tax revenues to substitute other taxes—most likely income taxes—for sales taxes. This is not as unthinkable as it might sound. As it is, the state sales tax base as a share of total personal income has been shrinking for some time. In 1980 it was a bit above 50 percent and by 2003 is projected to be down to 42 percent.[15] The main reasons for the erosion are the growth of mail-order sales, the rising share of services (which are not usually covered by sales taxes) in national output, and the steady expansion of legislative exemptions to sales taxes. If the decline in the sales tax base accelerates because of a rapid increase in e-commerce sales, some, perhaps many, jurisdictions might be tempted to act on their own, replacing the revenue with other sources, without waiting for interstate compacts or federal legislation. Because sales taxes generally are more regressive than income taxes, the net result of such a shift could make the overall tax system more progressive than the existing one.

One can imagine, however, that further ramifications might have the opposite effect. Shifting the reliance of states and localities from sales to income taxation might strengthen the case of those who would like to see the federal government reduce its income tax in favor of a national sales tax or value added tax. Since the federal government can tax sales wherever they occur, a federal sales or value added tax would automatically solve the problem of treating e-commerce and other sales equally. Some argue that substitution of consumption taxes for income taxes would enhance saving—a result about which we are skeptical—but the outcome in any event would also likely be a less progressive overall tax system.

All of these approaches would remove the tilt the current tax situation gives to e-commerce. Equalizing the tax burden might be expected to slow the growth rate of retail e-commerce slightly from what it would be under the current system, but this would not significantly slow the pace at which the main benefits from the Internet would be realized. That is because those benefits are likely to accrue overwhelmingly from the cost savings that firms reap from changing their modes of operation, rather than from increasing the volume of retail e-commerce.

If the sales tax for all goods transactions were eliminated, however, there would be a slight increase in purchases of goods relative to services, and this would enhance e-commerce in goods. But this effect most likely would be small and could easily be offset by the slight decline in services (including services sold over the net).

Broadband Policy

If you want broadband Internet service at home, you may be very frustrated. You may have ordered DSL service from an independent provider only to find that the provider delays coming to your house to install the service, all the while blaming the local telephone company for failing to coordinate the visit. Or you may already have bought DSL service from one such provider but learned later that it went bankrupt. Business failure has not been a problem for the Regional Bell Operating Companies (RBOCs), but slow responsiveness certainly has been. Many customers who want DSL from them are simply "on hold." Consumers are not alone in their frustration. Business complaints about the quality of telecommunications service generally are larger in number and have been growing far more rapidly than those lodged by consumers.[16]

Customers of cable broadband seem to have fared better; at least, cable leads DSL in the broadband race, with roughly double the subscriber base. Nonetheless, the proverbial wait for the "cable guy" to install or fix systems in homes has become part of the popular culture. Moreover, as with DSL service, cable broadband service is still unavailable in many parts of the country.

It wasn't supposed to be this way. In 1996 Congress enacted the Telecommunications Reform Act to stimulate competition in the industry between local and long-distance providers of telecommunications services, between new local service providers and incumbent Bell monopolies, and between cable and telecommunications companies. The Federal Communications Commission (FCC) was given authority to ensure that new competitors that needed to interconnect with the Bell monopolies or to share their lines would be able to do so. Yet so far, only a very small portion of this pro-competition agenda has come to pass. New competitive local exchange carriers (CLECs) and the long-distance companies have made only limited inroads into the local telecommunications business. At this writing, several of the CLECs have gone out of business, blaming the RBOCs and more recently the FCC for frustrating their efforts to compete. Although broadband now reaches about 7 million homes, the basic infrastructure is capable of handling vastly greater volume. Indeed, at this writing, there is so much excess fiber capacity in the trunk lines, or backbone infrastructure, that many telecommunications companies face the prospect of bankruptcy or, at best, weak profits for years to come. This is especially true in Europe, where telecommunications companies collectively have paid roughly $100 billion for new "3G" licenses to provide wireless Internet services. [17]

The main challenge for policymakers, who clearly want to remove any artificial roadblocks to the deployment of broadband, is to ensure that sufficient competition exists among the various providers of broadband service so that each has an adequate incentive to respond to user demand. The challenge is complicated because, for all intents and purposes, only two technologies for delivering broadband are likely in the foreseeable future: cable and DSL. Broadband Internet service by satellite, which has a much higher upfront cost for the dish, is still in its infancy.[18]

Under current law, the RBOCs are required to lease out their facilities at rates and on other terms set by regulators to independent service providers (ISPs), but cable providers are not subject to the same requirement. As we write this, a debate is raging in Congress and at the FCC about whether this imbalance in regulatory treatment ought to be corrected, with the objective of promoting more competition and thus accelerating the rollout of broadband by reducing its price and improving service by the carriers. Broadly speaking, there are three very different approaches for doing this, and all are controversial.

One path is to require each of the broadband providers—cable, telecommunications, and perhaps even satellite companies—to lease their lines to competitors, who can then resell the service. In essence, this "open-access" approach would treat all broadband providers equally, imposing on each the model that is now in place just for local telephone companies.

A second alternative is to level the playing field in the other direction—that is, to free the RBOCs from existing open access and obligatory sharing requirements for their broadband services, which would be placed in a separate affiliate, and meanwhile keep other broadband providers (cable and satellite) free from open-access regulation. The regional Bells would continue, however, to be subject to open-access requirements, as well as price regulation, in their local telephone operations, so long as they maintain a dominant position in that line of business. This approach is embodied in a controversial legislative proposal offered by Republican Billy Tauzin, chairman of the House Commerce Committee, and John Dingell, the ranking Democratic member of that committee.

A third approach is to leave existing law exactly where it is: continue to require the RBOCs to provide open access, while not subjecting cable providers to the same requirement.

Which approach is more likely to stimulate aggressive competition for servicing consumers? This is not an easy question to answer, and from our perspective, each approach has its risks.

Competitors to the RBOCs argue vigorously for the open-access regime, pointing to the existence of so many independent service providers as living proof of the power of competition. Advocates of the unregulated approach, however, note that unlike telephone service, which already is a monopoly, broadband is an entirely new service, whose market structure is uncertain. Cable may have a temporary lead now, but that situation may not last if the RBOCs are unleashed from existing sharing requirements for DSL service (which the RBOCs argue discourages their investment in the service), and as satellite technology continues to improve.

Supporters of the existing approach can argue that regulatory parity is not appropriate as long as there is a difference in the degree of competition to which the RBOCs and cable providers are exposed. Despite the rise of the CLEC industry, the RBOCs continue to have at least 90 percent shares of their overall markets and nearly 100 percent of the residential market, which is the one to which broadband applies. In effect, consumers in virtually all areas of the country still have no real choice in local telephone service. In contrast, many, if not most, consumers can choose between their local cable company and one of the satellite services for multichannel television services. Accordingly, at least for now, cable companies are probably less able to overcharge their current customers to subsidize new broadband service than is the case for the telephone companies.

What are decisionmakers to do? One way to think about answering this question is to ask and answer another: what are the dangers under each policy of guessing wrong? Under an open-access or regulated regime, policymakers may stimulate greater competition in the business of signing up broadband customers and servicing them thereafter, but at the potential cost of discouraging the owners of the underlying infrastructure—the cable, satellite, and telecommunications companies—from building out their networks. In addition, imposing open access runs a real risk of freezing current technology by giving those who lease the service the potential ability to complain about unfairness if and when the underlying service is changed in some significant respect. Under deregulation policymakers sacrifice some vigorous competition at the retail end but provide maximum incentives for build-out and innovation. Meanwhile, the current policy may provide insufficient incentives to the RBOCs to accelerate their deployment of broadband, but at least it does not sacrifice competition for those who now lease lines from the RBOCs (many of whom are complaining about the terms on which they accept those leases).

Our inclination at this point, and that is all it is, is that keeping the status quo—maintaining the existing difference in regulatory treatment of cable and DSL—minimizes the risk of adverse outcomes. Policymakers may well want to keep in mind the experience with cellular telephone service, which started out by law as a duopoly—only two carriers were authorized in each area, one of them an RBOC—but then became far more competitive in the mid-1990s when the government allowed the auction of three additional cellular licenses, bringing the total number of competitors up to five. The enhanced competition led to a drop in prices, a proliferation of service plans, and a significant increase in the numbers of people using cellular phones. Indeed, it is almost impossible to walk down the street these days, or drive a car, without seeing others talking on their wireless phones (the use in cars is not necessarily a welcome event). The risk of adopting something like the Tauzin-Dingell approach is that the broadband industry could quickly collapse to something like the pre-1990s cellular phone industry, with only two effective providers of broadband: the local RBOC and the local cable monopoly. That outcome, it seems to us, is one that the cellular phone experience suggests be avoided. If and when local telephone service becomes significantly more competitive, or if satellite and terrestrial point-to-point Internet service really takes off, we would then feel more comfortable deregulating all providers—and not imposing a leasing requirement.

Of course, we could be wrong about all this. One of the problems with making policy in a field of rapid technological change is that the assumptions upon which policy is made can be quickly outdated. So if, for example, one of the broadband technologies becomes so ubiquitous as to become another monopoly, then the case for an open access—or mandatory leasing requirement and accompanying regulation—becomes compelling. In the meantime, however, we are inclined to leave policy where it is and let the market mature before making radical changes that could have potentially significant detrimental effects.

Antitrust

The discussion of broadband policy serves as a reminder of how important competition policy can be to the diffusion of Internet technology (and indeed of *any* technology). Perhaps a more powerful illustration is the breakup of AT&T, which once monopolized telephone service throughout the United States.

The Justice Department brought suit against AT&T in 1974 for abusing its monopoly power by, among other things, refusing to interconnect long-distance competitors with AT&T's local telephone exchanges. It is now widely recognized that by breaking up AT&T, the government helped unleash a powerful wave of innovation in customer devices used with the telephone network, such as different types of telephones, answering machines, and fax machines. Of even greater importance, the breakup stimulated innovation in the network itself, which now consists largely of fiber optic cable, a technology that AT&T had several decades ago but did not deploy rapidly until the breakup unleashed long-distance competitors. Sprint and MCI, for example, used the deployment of fiber optics as a competitive advantage. Their lead forced AT&T to keep pace.

The natural question arises, therefore, how might anticompetitive practices frustrate the use and diffusion of Internet-related technologies? The estimated cost savings from the Internet that we have identified flow largely from the more intensive *use* of Internet software and hardware already in place. So it is difficult to imagine how this process could be frustrated—at least in the short to medium run—by collusion among firms in the Internet-producing sector of the economy, including software firms and telecommunications companies. Firms in certain sectors of the economy (including firms in Internet-related industries) could, of course, collude to set prices, divide markets, and engage in other activities punishable under the antitrust laws and, in the process of collusion, reduce their own efforts at cutting costs and implementing productivity-enhancing changes that the Internet makes possible. But this kind of behavior is unrelated to the Internet itself and is the one area of antitrust law on which there is broad consensus that enforcement must continue to be vigorous.

One aspect of the Internet, however, has raised some antitrust concerns: the development of business-to-business (B2B) exchanges operated by competitors, such as the recently announced joint venture of major automobile manufacturers (Covisint) and similar B2B exchanges in the chemical, steel, and other industries. These exchanges have been formed to make it easier for the participating firms to purchase supplies from various sources. The antitrust concern is whether the exchanges might also facilitate coordination of prices or exclusion of some buyers or sellers and thus impede competition.

This potential problem can probably be addressed through putting conditions on the way exchanges operate. At a minimum, price quotes on the exchanges should be "firm," not merely forecasts or suggestions of what suppliers might charge in the future. If the latter are permitted, the exchanges could serve as vehicles for price signaling, which can facilitate coordination of prices. That was what the Justice Department charged the major airlines had done in the early 1990s when they used the computer reservation system to post intended, rather than actual, fares. The airlines agreed to abandon that practice—and thus to post only "firm" prices—in a consent decree. Another concern is that exchanges could become "essential facilities." That is, they could become so important to the ordering of goods and services in particular markets that suppliers or consumers could find it difficult to do business in any other way. To eliminate that concern, the exchanges should be prohibited from arbitrarily precluding either buyers or sellers who might want to join. The same due process rules now apply to trade associations, and they can and should easily be applied to the exchanges.

Antitrust authorities must also be vigilant in preventing two other ways in which competition may be stifled in the high-tech sector, specifically in the telecommunications, computer hardware, and computer software industries. One is through mergers that lead to undue concentration of particular markets. The other is through anticompetitive conduct of dominant firms in a mar-

ket. Although these are both standard antitrust problems appli-
cable to all industries, one feature of the Internet and the industries related to it poses special antitrust enforcement challenges,
and antitrust scholars, enforcement officials, and judges have not
yet reached a consensus on how to meet those challenges.

Here we refer to the tendency toward "natural monopoly," or
"tipping," in some high-tech markets.[19] Several well-known
examples exist: the VHS format for videocassettes, Microsoft's
dominance of operating systems for personal computers, and
Intel's dominance of microprocessers for PCs. In each case, the
market tended toward a single supplier. The primary reason was
not the one long thought to cause natural monopolies in industries, such as telephones and electricity, where the fixed costs of
serving customers were so high, relative to the size of the market,
that only one firm could survive. Instead, the new markets have
tipped toward monopoly because of the "network effects" applying to the standards that the firms in these markets have established. The more people who used the standard, the greater
incentives suppliers—film producers (for videocassettes), applications software developers (for operating systems), and computer manufacturers (for microprocessors)—had to use it.
Network effects can also be reinforced by "lock-in" effects, which
arise when consumers invest the time and resources in becoming
familiar with one standard and thus incur high costs if they switch
to another one. In short, when a firm develops a technology that
becomes a standard in an industry, the firm acquires a monopoly.

What is the role of antitrust enforcement in such markets? It
is certainly not to prevent the development of standards, which

are valued by consumers and firms in related industries. The essential role for the authorities instead is to ensure that the market remains open to the development and use of *new* standards over time. This is not as simple as it sounds, however. Firms that already have a monopoly over a standard have a significant advantage over newcomers. Not only do they enjoy the benefits of consumer lock-in, but because they also are likely to know best the inner workings of the technology that has become the standard, they always have a built-in lead-time advantage over competitors in upgrading the standard and ensuring that any new technology is compatible with the old one (sometimes called "backward compatibility"). Incumbents do have one significant disadvantage, however. Precisely because they already have a monopoly, they may not have the incentive to keep pace with the market and develop upgrades or new standards. AT&T's delay in building out fiber optic cable is an excellent example.

It is not the job of antitrust enforcers to decide how this balance of incentives plays out in individual markets. But it is their job, as the prosecution of AT&T demonstrated, to prevent existing monopolies from abusing their market power to prevent the entry of rivals. Similarly, the Justice Department brought suit against Microsoft in the 1990s on two occasions for engaging in such practices. The first suit was settled in 1994. At this writing, the status of the second suit is unclear: although Microsoft lost the highly publicized trial and the follow-on appellate ruling, the case has been reassigned to a new judge, who is considering what remedies should be imposed to correct the antitrust violations.

Microsoft is not alone in attracting the attention of the antitrust officials. In the 1990s, the Federal Trade Commission charged Intel with abusing its dominance in microprocessors, a suit that was settled. It will be key for antitrust agencies in the future to ensure that dominant firms in markets subject to network externalities and lock-in do not abuse their power. Otherwise, firms in this position can frustrate innovation and thus slow the rate of productivity improvement upon which the continued advance in living standards depends.

The Role of Technology

Finally, the nature of what is available on the Internet can and almost certainly will affect the magnitude of its benefits. In this connection, knowledgeable observers of the net may wonder why we did not include among the sectors analyzed the so-called "content" industry: the distribution of sound and video recordings, as well as software, over the Internet.

In principle, both the quantifiable and unmeasurable benefits of Internet distribution of content are likely to be quite significant to the performance of the economy. Content can be sent in a flash to consumers, without diskettes and CDs having to be produced, stored, shipped, and displayed; the cost savings that could result are potentially sizable. Likewise, consumers can gain virtually instant access to the material without going to a store or having to wait for mail delivery.

There is a simple reason, however, why we excluded these potential savings. In the wake of the "peer-to-peer" computing revolution begun by Napster, the once immensely popular sound-recording file-sharing service, uncertainty is enormous about the magnitude of future content distribution over the Internet. Of course, Internet distribution is already significant for newspapers and magazines and even more so for pornographic material, but a large question mark surrounds the future of net-based delivery of sound or video recordings. At this writing, the courts have sharply curtailed the functionality of Napster and may in the future even force it to shut down. The "Napster cat" appears to be out of the bag, however. Already, equivalents of Napster have shown up on servers located outside the United States and thus apparently out of reach of U.S. law. Also available are legitimate services, such as Aimster, Bearshare, Gnuttella, KaZaA, among others, that do not compile a directory of content, but instead merely provide programs that can be downloaded onto an individual's computer. These services are very likely not in violation of U.S. copyright law—and even if they were, would society tolerate the police coming into literally millions of homes to inspect personal computers?

The music and software industries, some firms even in conjunction with Napster itself, nonetheless are trying to fight back with new technologies that make copying files without permission much more difficult, if not impossible.[20] Whether these technologies will remain impervious to "hacking" remains an open question. Just as important, it is not clear how much consumers will pay for recordings (sound and video) delivered over the Internet in different formats. If the new technologies work and people are willing to pay for them, then the benefits of net-based content distribution could be even more substantial than they already are—but it is too early to make that call.

Of course, even with the best of "digital rights management" technologies—those that prevent the unauthorized retransmission or copying of copyrighted works—the Internet, for technical reasons, may not be a reliable delivery mechanism for videos or interactive games for a long time. Even with broadband, downloading a video file still can take a while. Consumers may find it simpler and more convenient to keep ordering their movies from cable or satellite television. In addition, the quality of Internet-delivered video still is not nearly as high as it is on conventional television.

In fact, the notion of video-by-Internet raises even broader economic problems. Unlike television, where the cost of adding another customer is essentially zero, the costs of delivering video by streaming technologies to additional customers are measurable, although they may decline with more users hooked to the network. Licensing fees must be paid to the firms that enable the content to be seen—for example, to companies such as Real Networks, Apple, and Microsoft. Internet service providers also charge for carrying traffic to additional customers. For these reasons, and perhaps others, video streaming currently is used primarily to advertise television shows, not to replace them. It is far from clear that this will change in the near or long term.[21]

One final note: whatever one may think about Napster, one undeniable benefit of its technology is that it has so far acted as the main stimulant for demand for broadband. Music can be downloaded far faster with a broadband connection, in as little as a minute, than with the best modem, where a ten-minute wait is common. The speed with which some of the benefits of the Internet may be delivered has been accelerated, ironically, by what once was (and for many still is) a "renegade" technology.

6 *Concluding Thoughts*

THE INTERNET, LIKE most major innovations, has attracted more than its share of boosters. The overblown rhetoric of some of these enthusiasts depicts the Internet as revolutionizing almost all aspects of human life. Some have claimed the Internet will lead to unlimited prosperity, the end of the business cycle, and entirely new configurations of industry and commerce. This hyperbole has provoked skeptics into countering that the Internet is unlikely to have any significant effects at all. Our analysis, not surprisingly, has led us to a middle position. The impact of the Internet is unlikely to be either as overwhelming as some cyber-enthusiasts claim or as insignificant as the skeptics allege.

There are plenty of reasons to believe that the impact of the Internet on the economy will be important and lasting. We have summarized the Brookings study team's conclusions that use of the Internet will produce significant cost savings in many sectors of the economy. Some of these cost savings will result in faster productivity growth for some years in the future. Others will be reflected in narrower profit margins and lower prices for consumers. Overall, the Internet will improve living standards for average Americans.

Moreover, the Internet is likely to generate a wide variety of other benefits to consumers and citizens, which are not easily quantified but nonetheless real: savings in time, added convenience, increased choices, and the ability to find specialized or customized products and services without huge investments in searching for the right thing. Especially in an era when people are increasingly aware of the preciousness of time, these benefits may be far more noticeable and appreciated than the numbers that economists can more easily count.

Nevertheless, in 2001, when much of this book was being written, mention of the economic effect of the Internet provoked skeptical rolling of the eyes and snorts of disbelief. The NASDAQ stock price index, which is heavily weighted with companies in the information technology industry, was plunging far below its peak values of a year earlier, as shown in figure 6-1. A large part of that meltdown occurred among the dot.com stocks—stocks of companies with innovative ideas for commercial exploitation of the Internet's potential. A great many such companies were launched in the late 1990s amid high hopes for large sales and eventual profitability. They were lavishly supported by venture capitalists, who then tried to recoup their investment—with a big profit margin—by offering the stocks to the public, often before the company had a solid business plan, let

Figure 6-1. *Monthly Stock Index Closing Value,*
January 1996–present

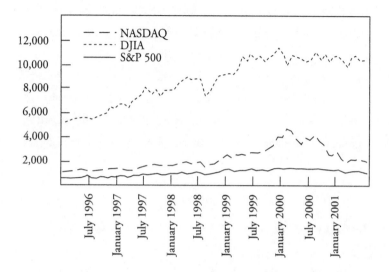

alone any convincing evidence of profits to be generated in the foreseeable future. Many of the dot.com stocks are no longer listed on any stock exchange, and many of the companies are out of business.

For those who thought the economic impact of the Internet was going to show up in profits and more valuable stocks—and stock options—for dot.com shareholders and employees, the bloom is off the Internet rose. In retrospect, many disappointed owners of dot.com stocks now view the vaunted Internet revolution as a craze, a mania, a reflection of irrational exuberance.

At the height of the hyperbole over the new economy in the late 1990s, some observers were proclaiming that information technology—especially cheap, instantaneous communication over the Internet—had abolished the business cycle. Companies would be so well informed about the needs of their customers that they would no longer experience back orders, accumulate excess inventory, or get caught with too little or too much productive capacity to satisfy consumer demand. At the same time, others were predicting, even before the economy slowed at the end of 2000, that the Internet could make economic cycles worse.

The claims and counterclaims are confusing. In this concluding chapter we attempt to straighten them out and offer our own views.

Beyond the Dot.coms

Unquestionably, the bubble phase of the Internet stock craze was characterized by irrational exuberance. Many companies that received generous infusions of capital on little more than an idea written on a napkin would never have been funded by venture capitalists focused on realistic earnings prospects or been successful in marketing their stock to the public in less frenzied times. There was so much blind faith in the future of anything even vaguely connected with the Internet that venture capitalists competed to give money to companies with sketchy ideas and rushed to sell their stock in markets loaded with buyers eager to get in on the latest "new new thing."

It was never realistic to imagine that physical commerce was going to be replaced in the manner and at the speed that some of the early Internet pioneers were claiming. It was crazy to think that the new economy would sweep away the old economy—the 90 percent or so of goods and services produced outside the tech sector broadly defined.

But beneath the exaggerated stories told about the new economy, there were and still are important nuggets of truth. The productivity surge of the late 1990s reflected the cumulative impact of high-tech investment, albeit not yet of the Internet. Huge investments in computers and telecommunications, which in recent years have accounted for about *half* of all investment in plant and equipment in the United States, would not have been made unless those raising and spending the funds believed that the investments would make a difference. And as we discussed in chapter 2, the best evidence is that by the mid-1990s they *did* make a difference.

The Brookings Task Force on the Internet addressed the next stage of the revolution and asked the question: What contribution to productivity growth can be expected from increasing use of the Internet over the next five years? The task force identified significant potential productivity gains likely to flow from growing use of the net, but these benefits were not based on the dot.coms adding huge value to the economy. In fact, we now know (and could have guessed before) that they would never do this. Instead, the productivity benefits of the Internet will be realized because of what firms and users in *the rest of the economy* do with the new technology. The magnitude of the benefits will depend on how people use this new ability to communicate rapidly and inexpensively with potentially millions, if not billions, of others around the globe. In short, the benefits of the Internet lie "beyond the dot.coms."

In this respect, the Internet is not inherently different from electricity, the telephone and telegraph, railroad, the airplane, or the automobile. Each of these watershed innovations were celebrated in their day because of what users could do with them: turn on lights, speak or communicate over long distances, or travel at speeds and in comfort that far surpassed the means previously possible. Similarly, when each of the innovations were brought to market, hundreds, in some cases thousands, of firms initially attempted to reap commercial benefits from providing these new services to consumers. As in the recent Internet stock craze, some of these new companies offered stock to a gullible public seeking to cash in on the latest technological wave. Most investors, however, were hugely disappointed. Most of the companies that went public and virtually all of them that remained private eventually fell by the wayside, victims of bad management, economies of scale, and effective competition from the leaders in the field. Relatively few firms exist in these industries today.

Would any serious observer claim that the demise of so many of the enterprises that helped launch the electricity, communications, and transportation revolutions somehow "proved" that the technologies they attempted to exploit and market were not important? Of course not. As the great Harvard economist Joseph Schumpeter persuasively argued, one of the hallmarks of a competitive market economy is that it is characterized by "creative destruction." The new and successful firms are constantly displacing the old ones. Failure is as much a feature of competition—and risk-taking—as success.

The bursting of the Internet stock bubble, then, differs little from previous stock market bubbles. Many of the companies that helped pioneer the Internet may be dead, but the technology they helped to develop and were endeavoring to exploit lives on. Users of the Internet will reap its benefits, and there is every reason to believe that these benefits eventually will be substantial.

At the same time, we suspect that the subject of this book—the benefits of the Internet—soon will be viewed as outdated. Does anyone read books any more about the benefits of electricity, the telephone, the automobile, or the airplane? We don't know about you, but we certainly don't. The reason is not hard to understand. Each of these technologies eventually became so intertwined with the rest of the economy that individuals and firms forgot that they were once special. The same will happen with the Internet, and indeed with the new and old economies more broadly. Workers who once thought they'd get rich in the dot.com sector have since been moving out to help old economy firms adapt to the Internet age (while earning lower, but more stable salaries in the process). Meanwhile, in product markets, the new and old will blend seamlessly together—"clicks with bricks," as many said just a short while ago—and it will no longer make sense to distinguish between the two. At that point, the economy will truly have moved beyond the dot.coms.

The Internet and the Business Cycle

In the halcyon days of the Internet craze—as recently as 1999, for example—some claimed that the Internet would usher in a new economic age, not only because it would lead to vast improvements in productivity, but because it would change the very nature of economic behavior. The main reason: the rapid flow of information made possible by the net would prevent the buildup of excess inventories or excess capacity in firms. Things would be made to order. No spare supplies or unsold goods would be sitting on shelves gathering dust (nor would firms be paying costly interest on loans to finance those goods). No redundant workers or managers would be drawing pay without producing. Companies would be operating "just in time," "lean and mean," or else they would not survive. The business cycle would disappear, or at least downturns would be less serious than in the past.

Two economists at Goldman-Sachs, William Dudley and Edward McKelvey, coined the term "brave new business cycle" in 1997. They pointed to a combination of structural, technological, and behavioral changes in the modern economy, including globalization, information technology, just-in-time management of payrolls and capacity as well as inventories, plus deregulation and improved fiscal and monetary policy responses. They believed these factors in combination were likely to increase productivity, reduce inflationary pressures, and reduce the frequency of business downturns, "making long-lived economic expansions the rule rather than the exception."[1] Dudley and McKelvey also noted that "longer bashes are likely to lead to bigger hangovers," because greater leverage could mean more financial distress in a downturn and require more aggressive monetary policy to get the economy moving up again.

These hopes were reminiscent of similar optimism in the long growth period of the 1960s. Then, some economists believed that government policymakers had learned how to fine tune the economy through prompt adjustments in fiscal or monetary policy to prevent inflation from accelerating or to stop a temporary increase in unemployment from snowballing into recession. They believed that if recession threatened, tax and interest rates could be cut and government expenditures raised in time to head off the worst of the downturn, and that the opposite policies could slow the economy in time to head off recession.

The optimists of the 1960s have been proved partly right. At least, no economic disaster of the magnitude and pervasiveness of the Great Depression of the 1930s has occurred since then. The relative stability of the economy for the past half century is at least partly attributable to a larger government serving as a counter-weight to fluctuations in the private sector and to the increased sophistication and technical skill of policymakers. Nevertheless, the business cycle emphatically did not disappear. Indeed, faced with slow growth and inflation at the same time, or stagflation, policymakers in the 1970s found themselves unable to use fiscal and monetary policy to get the economy back on the track.

An economy is a complex organism, especially one as large as that in the United States, where $10 trillion of goods and services are now produced and consumed each year. Although many aspects of the behavior of consumers and firms are predictable, many are not, and it is the unexpected shifts in sentiment, expressed through changes in demand for goods and services, that make economic forecasting so difficult. In such an environment, it would be a mistake to expect the Federal Reserve, Congress, and the executive branch all to anticipate—and always to correctly offset—any unexpected shifts in demand. This is certainly the case for the political branches of the government, especially Congress, which make decisions through the hard pull and tug of competing interests, of which macroeconomic stability is just one objective. In short, the business cycle did not die in the 1960s, as some might wishfully have thought, but instead made itself very evident on one major occasion in each of the subsequent decades.

The hopes of the 1990s that the information age would mitigate economic fluctuations may also prove partly right, but it has clearly not eliminated the business cycle altogether. As this book was being completed in the fall of 2001, economic growth in the United States had slowed sharply from its previous and unsustainable pace of about 4 percent during the previous year to almost no growth at all, and after the terrorist attack in September there was a consensus that the economy would slip into recession. The NASDAQ composite index at one point had fallen by more than 70 percent in value from its peak in March 2000, driven heavily by even more dramatic declines in the stock prices of high-tech and Internet companies. Strikingly, the earlier optimism about the brevity of the downturn seemed to have faded, replaced by a new pessimism about the fate of the tech sector generally, as well as the dot.coms. Rather than experiencing a short inventory correction, the economy, in the view of some, was appearing to suffer from a glut in capacity, confined not only to high-tech industries but evident more broadly throughout the manufacturing sector; it was feared that this excess capacity would dampen investment spending for some time to come. Although consumer spending held up remarkably well through the summer, analysts feared consumers would lose their faith, especially after the events of September. Layoffs, already heavy in manufacturing, could deepen in the service sector, and consumers might cut spending more drastically in response to heavy debt loads and losses suffered in the stock market. To make matters worse, economic growth elsewhere around the world also was slowing, dampening the demand for U.S. exports. Not only was the bloom off the Internet rose, but the flowers in the rest of the economic garden also seemed to be wilting.

As we write, the jury is still out on how soon the economy will recover and how strong the recovery will be. The dramatic slowing of economic growth that began at the end of 2000 and turned into a recession in the fall of 2001 may prove to be temporary, with growth resuming by 2002. The technology and skills of the information age may well prove helpful in stabilizing the economy more quickly than would have been possible in previous decades. If this happens, those who believed in the "brave new business cycle" will have increased credibility.

Alternatively, if the slowdown proves to be the prelude to a prolonged period of stagnation or even a serious recession, increased attention will be given to the role the Internet may have played in this shift in economic fortune. In particular, did the growing use of the net not only fail to mitigate the severity of the downturn, but even make it worse?

Michael Mandel, the business editor of *Business Week*, has outlined one of the more cogent cases for the proposition that the Internet, or more precisely, the enthusiasm with high tech more broadly, has made things worse, in his aptly titled book *The Coming Internet Depression* (released with good timing in the late spring of 2000, several months before the slowdown).[2] Mandel is by no means a skeptic about the importance of the Internet. Indeed, he is among the optimists about the long-run impact of the Internet and the high-tech revolution in raising productivity. But he voices much darker views about the interconnection of the high-tech boom and the rest of the economy in the short run when the economy seems to stumble, as it did beginning in late 2000.

Briefly stated, Mandel argues that the Internet and high-tech revolutions were made possible largely by venture capital financing. Once a relatively meager source of funds, venture capitalists by the end of the 1990s were pouring $100 billion a year into new ventures, many of them Internet-related. These investors, in turn, were depending on the continuing rise in the stock markets, especially the NASDAQ where the new high-tech issues predominantly were traded, to "liquefy" their investments in startups through initial public offerings of stock. The rise of the dot.coms dramatically lowered barriers to entry in many lines of business, scaring large numbers of old economy firms in the process. This fear of being displaced, in Mandel's view, propelled firms throughout the economy to improve productivity, which kept inflation in check and thus allowed the Federal Reserve to feel comfortable with a steadily falling unemployment rate; under other circumstances the steady decline in joblessness might have triggered fears that wage pressures would lead to an acceleration in inflation and thus have led the Fed to tighten monetary policy in anticipation of that possibility.

All of this was well and good as long as demand for goods and services was strong, because the high-tech sector, the venture capital industry, and the economy as a whole were caught up in a virtuous circle. But prick the bubble in the stock market—as occurred in March 2000—and all of the forces for good that Mandel identifies on the economy's way up would make things much worse on the way down. Mandel feared that the realization that firms had invested too heavily in capacity and thus would soon suffer a significant drop in profits, or at least a sharp slowing of their growth, would trigger a sinking stock market. That would send a chill through the venture capital community, which then would turn off the funding spigot for new high-tech ventures. Since, in Mandel's view, the dot.coms were a primary force driving up productivity, their disappearance from the scene would allow firms in the old economy to relax and to raise prices. This immediately would put the Fed in a bind, reminding the authorities of the stagflation of the mid-1970s when both inflation and unemployment jumped sharply. Mandel argues that the Fed, traditionally focused on the dangers of inflation, would then choose to fight inflation rather than the downturn and would raise interest rates, making the downward slide worse. Like a dog chasing its tail, the stock market would sink further; so would venture capital funding, and thus productivity growth. Eventually, an "Internet depression" would arrive.

Indeed, some elements in this narrative came to pass much as Mandel predicted. In retrospect, the bursting of the NASDAQ bubble probably was the first warning sign that economic growth eventually was going to falter. Venture capital funding did fall roughly in half over the following year. Many, if not most, of the dot.coms did die. Profits slumped sharply in early 2001. Many investors took it on the chin. Nevertheless, it would be a mistake, in our view, to conclude that the rest of the Mandel narrative— or more broadly, claims that the Internet somehow has widened the amplitude and lengthened the economic cycle—is necessarily fated to become reality.

For one thing, it is not plausible to attribute the remarkable surge in productivity growth in the last half of the 1990s to the competitive pressure of dot.com companies on old economy firms. The e-commerce revolution did not really begin until the end of the decade and even now remains in its infancy. Moreover, the productivity surge was not primarily driven by dot.coms threatening old-line companies, because e-business had not yet really taken off during this period (although Internet businesses applied some pressure in a few lines of business, such as online stock trading.) The demise of the dot.coms, therefore, should not significantly impair the future growth of productivity. To the contrary, as we noted earlier in the chapter, perhaps the main finding of the Brookings Internet study is that the Internet revolution promises to reform the *old economy*, not the dot.coms, which are (or were) change agents at best. There is every reason for believing that the Internet will continue to *add* to productivity growth, regardless of what happens to the NASDAQ.

Second, although it is not surprising that the venture capital industry would suffer when the stock bubble burst, it is noteworthy that even at an annual rate of $50 billion in new investment—which was about the rate at this writing—the industry is still roughly ten times its size of a decade ago. Now that the legal and financial infrastructure of venture capital financing has been built, it is highly unlikely to sink into oblivion. In any event, even the $50 billion drop in financing during the 2000–01 period represents a relatively small portion, about 5 percent, of total plant and equipment investment in the United States. To be sure, venture capital is higher-risk money, more like investment in research and development than new machinery or buildings. Nonetheless, it is important to keep the size of the industry in perspective before jumping to the conclusion that the economy must suffer some irreparable harm when the volume of funds coursing through venture capital firms takes a steep, but most likely temporary, nosedive. Moreover, it is our impression that a lot of money in the venture capital industry is waiting for the business climate to improve and so has not suddenly disappeared.

Third, the weakest link in the "Internet depression" scenario—especially with hindsight— is the forecast that the Federal Reserve would fail to loosen monetary policy when confronted with a weakening economy, for fear of stoking the fires of inflation. It is true that the consumer price index was rising at 4 percent in the first quarter of 2001 and even the so-called core rate of inflation (the percentage growth in the consumer price index minus the effects of the volatile food and energy sectors) was more than 3 percent. Nonetheless, early in 2001 the Fed began an aggressive series of interest rate cuts, even acting between the regularly scheduled meetings of the Federal Open Market Committee, a relatively rare event. Lower rates are the equivalent of a tax cut for borrowers, giving them more spending power. In addition, lower rates have helped brake the stock market's fall and thus helped keep consumption spending from weakening excessively. To be sure, lower rates probably will have a more difficult time stimulating investment, especially in high-tech, where excess capacity deters firms from making new big bets. In addition, at least through much of 2001, lower interest rates have not led to a weaker dollar, which would stimulate exports. Most likely that is because other economies in the rest of the world have been weak, and investors thus remain attracted to investing in this country and in dollar-denominated assets. Still, the monetary stimulus provided by the Fed, coupled with some help from the tax cut in 2001, should keep the 2000–01 economic slowdown from becoming a long slump, even in the wake of the economic anxieties generated in the aftermath of the terrorist attack on the United States in September 2001.

In short, the Internet enthusiasts who claimed that the Internet would somehow shorten, or even eliminate, economic cycles were probably wrong. But the pessimists were misplaced, too, to the extent they claimed that the Internet and the high-tech revolution more generally would inevitably lead to the opposite result. Business cycles, in particular, occasional downturns, are likely to be with us regardless of what technology may come along to enhance long-run productivity. Economic growth can slow or turn negative for a host of reasons, including unexpected shocks (such as large run-ups in energy prices), a tightening of fiscal or monetary policy in an effort to rein in inflation, or, as the most recent downturn demonstrates, because investments in capacity run too far ahead of demand. Each of these potential sources of economic trouble is likely to remain even in a world of ever faster communications made possible by the Internet.

More broadly, the advent of the Internet has not repealed the basic economic laws that governed the economy in the past and will continue to do so in the future. Perhaps there is no better example of this proposition than Cisco, one of the Internet pioneers whose cost-cutting experience with the net serves as the basis for our projections for cost-savings for the rest of the manufacturing sector. At one brief point during 2000, Cisco had the highest market valuation of any company in the world, even surpassing that of Microsoft. By spring 2001 Cisco's value had shrunk by roughly 80 percent, largely because the company's fast growth in revenues came to a sudden halt and then turned down. Cisco was not prepared for the reversal of fortune, having ordered substantial volumes of supplies to ensure that it could meet continued expected increases in demand for the company's routers and other Internet-related equipment. In the event, the growth in demand never materialized, and the company was forced to liquidate much of its inventory at steep losses.

Skeptics might naturally ask how this sequence of events could happen if the Internet was saving Cisco so much money in the form of lower inventory and transactions costs. To put it even more bluntly, is it possible that the alleged costs savings from the Internet never were real? The short answer to these questions is that the Internet can and almost certainly does help companies save money, but it does not insulate them from managerial mistakes. Even the best of expert systems cannot, and should not, eliminate human judgment. Sometimes humans guess wrong—even humans who run new economy companies. They order too much (or not enough, as the case may be). If enough firms, which are led by people after all, make mistakes at the same time, they can help tilt the economy's performance away from its optimal path. The Internet cannot and will not replace these boom-and-bust cycles in human behavior, nor was it ever realistic to suppose that it could. But the Internet can help companies save money doing whatever they do and however successful they may be in forecasting future demand.

Finally, what about the effect of the recession on the pace at which benefits from the Internet itself are likely to be realized (the subject of chapter 5)? The slowdown of overall economic growth in 2000–01 was accompanied by a sharp drop in spending for information technology goods and services, broadly defined, which in turn reduces the capital-deepening effect on productivity that IT has traditionally had. We are more sanguine, however, that the IT slowdown will not make a significant dent in the pace at which *Internet-related productivity gains* are likely to be realized. The major reason for our optimism is that the hardware and software required to "webify" companies generally is not a major constraint; the more important costs of Internet-related investments are "organizational," that is, the time and commitment senior management needs to shift current paper-based systems to existing technologies for ordering supplies and moving them through the "value chain" to generate finished products and services. It is thus quite conceivable that any overall economic downturn actually may intensify management interest in such cost-saving activities as a way of keeping profitability up (or at least not down too much) in a more difficult general economic climate. In this scenario, Internet-related productivity improvements may therefore be realized at a *faster* pace than otherwise during a wider economic slowdown.

But even if this favorable outcome does not materialize, it remains clear that the Internet stands as one of the more important innovations of the past several decades. Whether it will ultimately rank as one of the more important innovations of the last *century* remains an open question and one that we need not resolve here. All that we hope to have done is to convince readers that the economic benefits of the Internet—both quantifiable and nonquantifiable—are likely to be significant and grow over time. The benefits do not hinge on the survival of the dot.coms. Instead, they will accrue to firms and eventually to consumers through the transformation of business processes throughout the rest of the economy that the Internet is making possible. In short, there will be Internet life long after the dot.coms.

Notes

Chapter 1

1. Michael J. Mandel, *The Coming Internet Depression: Why the High-Tech Boom Will Bust, Why the Crash Will Be Worse Than You Think and How to Prosper from It* (Basic Books, 2000).

2. Brookings Task Force on the Internet, *The Economic Payoff from the Internet Revolution* (Brookings, 2001).

Chapter 2

1. Until the figures were revised in the summer of 2001, it appeared that the post-1996 productivity growth rate was close to the previous postwar high of about 3 percent.

2. Robert M. Solow, "We'd Better Watch Out," *New York Times Book Review,* July 12, 1987, p. 36.

3. Daniel E. Sichel, *The Computer Revolution: An Economic Perspective* (Brookings, 1997).

4. Stephen D. Oliner and Daniel E. Sichel, "Computers and Output Growth Revisited: How Big is the Puzzle?" *Brookings Papers on Economic Activity,* 1994 (2), pp. 273–334.

5. Robert J. Gordon, "Has the 'New Economy' Rendered the Productivity Slow-down Obsolete?" *Journal of Economic Perspectives*, vol. 14 (Fall 2000), pp. 49-74.

6. Council of Economic Advisers, *Economic Report of the President* (Government Printing Office, 2001), pp. 95–144.

7. Kevin J. Stiroh, "Investing in Information Technology: Productivity Payoffs for U.S. Industries," *Current Issues in Economic and Finance* (Federal Reserve Bank of New York), vol. 7, no. 6 (June 2001).

8. Paul A. David, "The Dynamo and the Computer: An Historical Perspective on the Modern Productivity Paradox," *American Economic Review*, vol. 80 (May 1990), pp. 355–61.

Chapter 3

1. Brookings Task Force on the Internet, *The Economic Payoff from the Internet Revolution* (Brookings, 2001).

2. There are skeptics that the Internet will produce much in the way of cost savings in health care. For such a view, see J. D. Kleinke, "Vaporware.com: The Failed Promise of the Health Care Internet," *Health Affairs* (November/December 2000), pp. 57–71.

3. The fact that Cisco has suffered financially throughout calendar 2001, reflected in the notable drop in its stock price, is not in any way inconsistent with the fact that the Internet almost certainly has enabled the company to realize cost savings (and thus stands to help other companies reduce costs as well). All the cost savings in the world will not generate additional profit if sales for a company's product drop significantly, as occurred in Cisco's case during the first months of 2001. See also chap. 6.

4. Martin Brooks and Zaki Wahaj, "The Shocking Economic Impact of B2B," Global Economic Paper 37, Goldman Sachs, New York, February 3, 2000.

Chapter 4

1. Eric J. Thomas and others, "Costs of Medical Injuries in Utah and Colordao," *Inquiry*, 36 (Fall 1999), pp. 255–64.

2. Of course, it is possible that the same benefits could be realized without the Internet if it turns out that patients record their histories on smart cards they carry with them rather than on centralized data bases that could be less secure and thus less private.

3. Robert D. Putnam, *Bowling Alone: The Collapse and Revival of American Community* (Simon and Schuster, 2000).

4. The discussion from here to the rest of the chapter draws on Robert E. Litan, "Law and Policy in the Age of the Internet," *Duke Law Journal*, vol. 50, no. 4 (February 2001), pp. 1045–86.

5. Andrew Shapiro, *The Control Revolution: How the Internet Is Putting Individuals in Charge and Changing the World We Know* (New York: Public Affairs Press, 1999).

6. Gary Burtless and others, *Globaphobia: Confronting Fears about Open Trade* (Brookings, 1998).

Chapter 5

1. U.S. Department of Commerce, *Digital Economy 2000,* June.

2. Melinda Patterson Grenier, "Web Access Extends to over 75% of U.S. Public-School Classrooms," *Wall Street Journal,* June 6, 2001, p. B2.

3. Quoted to the authors.

4. Severin Borenstein and Garth Saloner, "Economics and Electronic Commerce," *Journal of Economic Perspectives,* vol. 15, no. 1 (Winter 2001), pp. 3–12.

5. Matt Murray and Jathon Sapsford, "GE Reshuffles Its Dot.Com Strategy to Focus on Internal 'Digitizing,'" *Wall Street Journal,* May 4, 2001, p. B1.

6. For evidence that the business slowdown of 2001 has not kept companies from "webifying" their operations, see Leslie Walker, "Plugged in for Maximum Efficiency," *Washington Post,* June 20, 2001, pp. G1, G4; and Fred Vogelstein, "Flying on the Web," *Fortune,* April 30, 2001, pp. 142–46.

7. For an excellent guide to the issues relating to the next generation Internet, see "Upgrading the Internet," *Economist Technology Quarterly,* March 2001, pp. 32–36.

8. National Research Council, Computer Science and Telecommunications Board, *Trust in Cyberspace* (Washington: National Academy Press, 1998).

9. Toby Lester, "The Reinvention of Privacy," *Atlantic Monthly,* vol. 287, no. 3, (March 2001), pp. 27–39.

10. Federal Trade Commission, "Privacy Online: Fair Information Practices in the Electronic Marketplace: A Report to Congress" (www.ftc.gov/OS/2000/05 [May 2000]).

11. That risk is possible, if not encouraged, in the financial area at least. That is because the financial modernization legislation enacted in 1999, while broadening activity authority for financial holding companies and extending new privacy protections (largely an opt-out for some information to third parties), explicitly did not preempt potentially tougher state standards.

12. Austan Goolsbee, "Internet Commerce, Tax Sensitivity, and the Generation Gap," in James Porterba, ed., *Tax Policy and the Economy,* vol. 14 (MIT Press and NBER, 1999), pp. 45–66.

13. See Hal Varian, "Taxation of Electronic Commerce," in Internet Policy Institute, *Briefing the President* (Washington: Internet Policy Institute, April 2000), pp. 75–84.

14. During mid-2001, Senator John McCain offered a compact proposal, one that Congress would approve only after twenty-five of the forty-five states that now rely

on sales taxes had joined the compact. Upon approval, states would be able to compel merchants located in their jurisdictions to collect use taxes on purchases from out-of-state residents. At this writing, Congress is considering some form of this proposed legislation.

15. Donald Bruce and William J. Fox, "E-Commerce in the Context of Declining State Sales Tax Bases," *National Tax Journal*, vol. 52, no. 4, part 3 (2000), pp. 1373–88.

16. Shawn Young, "Complaints Rise as Phone-Service Problems Mount," *Wall Street Journal*, May 3, 2001, p. B, B4.

17. For an excellent survey of the problems confronting the industry, see Steve Rosenbush and Peter Elstrom, "8 Lessons from the Telecom Mess," *Business Week*, August 13, 2001, pp. 60–67.

18. Yuki Noguchi, "Slow to Take Off," *Washington Post*, August 8, 2001, pp. E1, E10.

19. For a much fuller explanation of this point, see Carl Shapiro and Hal Varian, *Information Rules: A Strategic Guide to the Network Economy* (Harvard Business School Press, 1999).

20. Microsoft, for example, has included an audio player in its new operating system, Windows XP, a system that does not use the MP3 format that heretofore has been widely used by consumers (and is easily subject to copying). Real Networks also is encouraging consumers to use its proprietary format rather than MP3, in conjunction with AOL Time Warner, while Sony is joining forces with Vivendi and Yahoo.

21. For further thoughts along these lines, see Claire Tristram, "Broadband's Coming Attractions," *Technology Review*, June 2001, pp. 70–75.

Chapter 6

1. William C. Dudley and Edward F. McKelvey, "The Brave New Business Cycle: No Recession in Sight," *U.S. Economic Research* (New York: Goldman Sachs, January 1997).

2. Michael J. Mandel, *The Coming Internet Depression: Why the High-Tech Boom Will Bust, Why the Crash Will Be Worse Than You Think and How to Prosper from It.* (Basic Books, 2000).

Index

33; profit margins cut by, 34–35.
See also Antitrust
Competitive local exchange carriers
(CLECs), 87, 89
Computers. *See* Information technol-
ogy; Software
Congress, 15, 86, 88
Consumers: benefits from Internet-
generated productivity growth,
34, 42; household Internet use,
66, 73; Internet auctions, 31;
medical information for, 54–55;
online shopping, 46–49; spend-
ing, 111, 116
Content distribution, 97–100
Convenience benefits of Internet,
46–49
Council of Economic Advisers, 13
Covisint, 93
Credit cards, 78
Cyber-communities, 59

Danzon, Patricia, 23
David, Paul A., 13–14
Dell Computer Corporation, 30, 37,
50
Democracy: Internet voting, 61–62;
representative, 62
Digital divide, 5–6, 66–68
Digital rights management technolo-
gies, 98–99
Digital Subscriber Lines. *See* DSL
Dingell, John, 89, 91
Distance learning, 27–28, 47
Dot.coms: boom, 2, 112; competi-
tion with traditional companies,
114; venture capital investments,
102–03, 104, 112. *See also* Stock

prices
DSL (Asynchronous Digital
Subscriber Lines), 72, 86, 88, 89
Dudley, William C., 108–09

eBay, 30, 31
E-commerce: B2B, 33, 34, 93–94;
choices, 49–51; competition with
traditional retailers, 40; convenience, 46–49; growth, 30–31;
international, 71; privacy issues,
77; and sales tax, 82–84; time
savings, 48; volume, 19
Economic performance: *1960*s, 109;
*1990*s, 14–15; predictions of
depression, 112–14; role of Internet, 111–12; slowdown in
2000–01, 16–17, 70, 110–11,
114; and terrorism, 17; unpre-
dictability, 109–10
Education: computers and Internet
access in schools, 67; distance
learning, 27–28, 47; productivity
growth from Internet, 39–40; of
workers, 9
Efficiency gains from Internet, 28–32
Elections: Internet voting, 61–62;
presidential (*2000*), 62
Electronic medical record, 24
Europe: telecommunications companies, 87

Federal Communications Commis-
sion (FCC), 87, 88
Federal Reserve Bank, 15, 16, 113,
115–16
Federal Trade Commission (FTC), 97
Financial services: brokers, 25–26;